THE Meditation OF YOGANANDA

THE Meditation OF YOGANANDA

A Handbook for Finding Inner Joy

Based on the Teachings of
PARAMHANSA YOGANANDA

Jayadev Jaerschky

CRYSTAL CLARITY PUBLISHERS   Nevada City, California

© 2022 Yogananda Edizioni
All rights reserved. Published 2022
Reissue of the first edition 2025
Printed in the United States of America

CRYSTAL CLARITY PUBLISHERS
crystalclarity.com / clarity@crystalclarity.com
14618 Tyler Foote Rd. / Nevada City, California
800.424.1055

ISBN 978-1-56589-111-1 (print) | 2025015615 (LOC print)
ISBN 978-1-56589-649-9 (e-book) | 2025015616 (LOC e-book)

Cover and interior design by Tejindra Scott Tully

Please note that the choice and the prescription of the right therapy are the sole responsibility of the treating physician, who can also assess any side effects. The information, preparations, recipes, exercises, and suggestions contained in this book have no therapeutic value. Therefore, the author and the publisher are not responsible for any damage or accidents resulting from the use of this information without the necessary medical supervision (self-treatment, self-medication, self-prophylaxis, etc.).

DEDICATION

In loving memory of
my spiritual teacher,
Swami Kriyananda,
who brought out the
true Self in each of us,
referring to us as
"a jewel, a saint, or
an angel."

I am deeply grateful to him
because, asked if he wanted
to check my manuscripts,
he simply answered:
"It's not necessary.
I trust Jayadev."

I dedicate this book to him,
hoping that his trust
was justified.

PARAMHANSA YOGANANDA in meditation.

CONTENTS

Preface *by Nayaswami Jyotish & Nayaswami Devi* ix

Introduction *by the author* xi

PART 1

Learning the *Hong-Sau* technique

1

Introduction to the ancient *Hong-Sau* Technique

3

Week 1 of Meditation Training: Preparation

17

Week 2 of Meditation Training: the BODY

27

Week 3 of Meditation Training: the MIND

35

Week 4 of Meditation Training: the SOUL

47

PART 2

Deepening your practice of the *Hong-Sau* technique

55

Introduction to Part 2: Meditation as a Lifestyle

57

Week 1 of Advanced Training: Going Deeper With *Hong-Sau*

65

Week 2 of Advanced Training: Non-Attachment

77

Week 3 of Advanced Training: Relaxation

83

Week 4 of Advanced Training: Contentment

89

Week 5 of Advanced Training:
Self-analysis
107

Week 6 of Advanced Training:
Radiating Blessings
119

Week 7 of Advanced Training:
Overcoming Dry-Spells
127

PART 3

Hong-Sau for Self-Realization
141

Introduction to Part 3:
Self-realization
143

Week 1 of Self-realization Training:
Hong-Sau Peaks
153

Week 2 of Self-realization Training:
Devotion
163

Week 3 of Self-realization Training:
Cooperating With Grace
175

Week 4 of Self-realization Training:
The Spiritual Eye
189

Week 5 of Self-realization Training:
Attunement
199

Week 6 of Self-realization Training:
Space
207

Week 7 of Self-realization Training:
Freedom
215

Conclusion 227

Index of Sources 229

EDITOR'S NOTE

As this book may be used by the reader as a basis for further study and investigation, the greatest possible attention was given to the source of each citation. However, in order not to render the reading burdensome, a simplified system was adopted by which the complete bibliographical reference is given only the first time that a source appears in the text. Subsequently, only the title of the source is given. The complete and detailed list of sources can be found on page 229.

PREFACE

by

Nayaswami Jyotish & *Nayaswami Devi*
~Spiritual Directors, Ananda Worldwide~

Breath is one of the great mysteries of life. Breathing is the first thing we do when we emerge into this world, and the last thing we do when we leave it. We begin with a cry and end with a sigh.

All mystical traditions teach techniques for using the breath to attain a more expanded consciousness. Watching the breath is a foundational practice in all schools of meditation, while using the breath in association with a prayer is used in mystical Christian teachings. In the yogic tradition, the breath is associated with both the flow of prana, or life-force, and with the mind. If we calm the breath, we are able to direct the life-force in the body which also calms restless thoughts.

In the teachings of yoga, breath is the cord that ties the soul to the body. If observing the breath is done with deep concentration, this simple technique can take us to the highest state of awareness. Paramhansa Yogananda, the father of yoga in the West, made it one of his central teachings.

Jayadev Jaerschky's book, *The Meditation of Yogananda*, explores this technique in great depth. In Yogananda's teachings, it is called *Hong-Sau* after the sound made by the inner flow of prana as we inhale and exhale.

The Meditation of Yogananda is a very practical guide since the value of any technique comes from its practice. Paramhansa Yogananda said amusingly, "If you go to a doctor to cure a disease and he hands you a prescription, it does no good to take it home, frame it, and hang it on the wall." The "prescription" in this book comes in the form of 18 weekly lessons. If you practice these techniques, it will help cure you of the disease of ignorance.

Some sage advice is that if you need to have a surgical procedure, it is best to go to a doctor who has performed thousands of them. Kriyacharya

Jaerschky has given thousands of classes during his lifetime as a yoga practitioner and teacher. If you are a beginner to meditation, this book will give you all the guidance you need to establish a daily practice. If you are an experienced meditator, you will find everything you need to take you deeper in your practice. For those who follow the teachings of Yogananda, this book is filled with quotes and advice from him and from his direct disciple, Swami Kriyananda.

The fruit of meditation is peace of mind and a joyful spirit at all times. In the Bhagavad Gita, it says, "Even a little practice of this inward religion (meditation) will save you from dire fears and colossal suffering." No matter what is going on around us, peace can be found within through watching the breath and calming the mind.

Though the times in which we live are filled with uncertainty and instability, we can rise above the storm. What better skill to develop now than to find greater assurance and strength within yourself through the practice of meditation. This book can be your guide.

INTRODUCTION

Dear Reader,

The basic impulse of life is to find happiness. You want it, I want it, everyone wants it, even the animals and plants want it.

The true happiness that we all want is by no means a small thing. If the yogic teachings are correct, it is the very essence of life, the essence of our soul, the core of our being. The Indian scriptures call it *Sat-chid-ananda*: existence-consciousness-bliss. Paramhansa Yogananda translated the term as "ever existing, ever conscious, ever new bliss."

We have lost it and are looking for it in so many different ways.

Indeed, if we ask ourselves what we want from life, we may come up with a specific answer: maybe money, success, fame, friendship, love, peace, etc.

But *why* do we want these things? Because we believe they will bring us to a state of happiness. Quite simply, what we all want is a happy life.

Happiness is, therefore, "the mother of all desires," because every single one of our countless desires stems from that prime and fundamental desire to be happy.

Scientists at this point might smile condescendingly and offer us an explanation concerning the "true" nature of happiness. They describe happiness as a purely neuro-chemical experience, as chemicals being released in our brain. There are four of them, they say, each of which produces a different sense of happiness in us: *dopamine, oxytocin, serotonin,* and *endorphin.*

- *Endorphin*-happiness is triggered by physical pain. It might be called the "pain-killer chemical."

- *Dopamine*-happiness is triggered when we get a new reward. It may be an ice-cream, or a victory, or finally obtaining what we want. It might be called the "achiever-chemical."

- *Oxytocin*-happiness is triggered when we trust those around us. It may be called the "relationship chemical."
- *Serotonin*-happiness is triggered when we feel valued or important. It might be called the "ego-chemical."

These four chemicals were developed a long time ago in our bodies because of primitive ancestral needs: the animals felt pain and needed immediate relief (*endorphin*); they saw their prey and wanted the reward (*dopamine*); they needed to feel good in the herd (*oxytocin*); and they needed to prevail (*serotonin*).

Yogis, however, give us a very different approach to the task of finding happiness. They say that its secret does not lie with any chemical or hormone, but that it is, as we said, the natural essence of our soul, *ananda,* and that it can be experienced by going deep in meditation.

In contrast to the short-lived effect of the four brain chemicals (and of drugs, alcohol, or adrenaline), soul-joy never diminishes. It is an eternal flame, lasting even longer than the one on Mount Chimaera in Yanartaş, Turkey, which has been burning for over 2,500 years and continues to burn today.

Yet if this is true, why do we not experience our inner eternal happiness?

Our problem is that we hold our consciousness on a level which is too superficial, which is fragile, dependent, and materialistic. On such a level, we simply do not have access to our innate joy, which can only be discovered by going deeply into the inner silence.

Once we feel it, floodgates automatically open, infusing our mind, our heart, our body and our whole life with the elixir of happiness.

Yogananda, therefore, advises us to affirm it, as if it were already ours:

"Happiness is the greatest divine birthright—
the buried treasure of my soul.
I have found that at last I shall secretly be rich
beyond the dream of Kings."
(From the *Praecepta Lessons*)

Advanced yogis, as, for example, was Swami Kriyananda, are our best role models for this way of life, because they constantly swim in a deep river of inner joy and share it with others. A simple song by Yogananda, consisting of only three words, expresses this inner state wonderfully: "Joy, joy, joy, ever-new joy."

But there is more to be said, for enlightened yogis teach that *ananda* (joy) is not only the true essence of all of us, but also the hidden essence of *all* creation. It is what is called "God," "the Absolute," or "pure eternal Consciousness."

Is all the above, however, just another form of belief? Yogic teachings have *never* been just a belief, a religion, or a theory. Rather, they call us to regular action, beginning NOW. "The proof of the pudding is in the eating," as the proverb says.

Speaking soul to soul: "Dear reader, may you meditate daily using the *Hong-Sau* technique so that your soul-joy will slowly surface. This book has no other purpose than to be a loving and practical guidebook for your inner journey toward happiness."

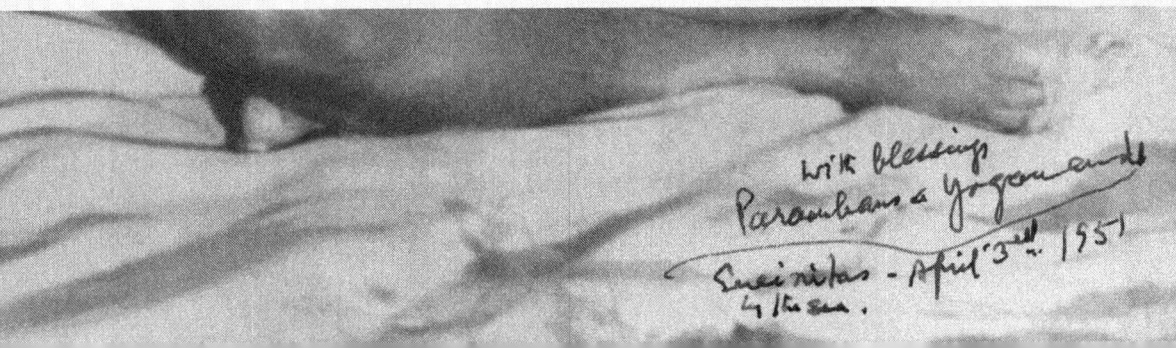

Part 1 | Learning the *Hong-Sau* Technique

sounds of the chakras and eventually the primordial vibration of OM. Three centuries ago, the *Gheranda Samhita* (3.77–81) described it using the name *Brahmari*: a technique used to perceive in the right ear the various subtle sounds. Already around 900AD, the *Goraksha-Paddhati* (11, 16) described the specific *mudra* (symbol) of the hands which helps to perceive these inner sounds.

Energization Exercises

Yogananda's third principal technique is less known but no less precious: the 39 *Energization Exercises*, which are his own personal creation. However, its method of directing energy in the body has a longstanding tradition: in olden times it was known as *prana dharana* (concentration of life-force), by which the yogis healed their body of various diseases. It is described for example in the *Tri-Shikhi-Brahmana-Upanishad* (11, 109), which explains how it conquers all illnesses and fatigue.*

Energization Exercises

Hong-Sau

The *Hong-Sau* technique also has an illustrious history. It has been cherished for centuries as the *Hamsa* technique and is considered a crest-jewel in the yogic scriptures. The *Svacchanda Tantra* (VII, 55) for example states: "The *sadhaka* (spiritual aspirant) who becomes absorbed in hamsa is a knower of the highest reality." *Hamsa*, Yogananda explained, is pronounced *"Hong-Sau."*

The title of this book, *The Meditation of Yogananda*, was chosen because *Hong-Sau* is an essential part of his teachings. In truth, however, it does not belong to Yogananda, but is a practice which has existed throughout the ages, being handed down from one generation to the next. It has been taught by enlightened yoga masters in slightly varying forms and has accompanied countless seekers toward the experience of inner depth, happiness, and Self-realization. Yogananda affirms that it "has been widely practiced in India for more than 7,000 years."†

---

* Ananda Yoga, "the yoga of Yogananda," is a style of Hatha Yoga, which is also rooted in the authentic Indian tradition. Swami Kriyananda, as he practiced the *asanas* (postures) in the presence of Yogananda, understood their original purpose: namely, to prepare the body and mind for meditation and Self-realization. Swami Kriyananda explained in a talk: "Ananda Yoga is really the ancient science and we are just trying to express it again clearly. So it's nothing that we can possess. It's just that our system, in a sense you might say by default, ought to be everybody's. It ought to be included and rather made the core of all Hatha Yoga teaching, because this is the essence of the ancient teaching."
† Yogoda Introduction, 1923.

The meaning of *Hong-Sau*

Hong-Sau is the mantric form of the Sanskrit words *aham-saha* (at times also transliterated as *aham-sa* or *aham-sah*), which literally means: "I am He."

Hamsa or *Hansa* (pronounced *Hong-Sau*) is the Sanskrit word for swan, which in India has always been a symbol for the immortal soul (*atman*). The *Hamsa Upanishad* (16) states: "Like the fire, invisibly present in the wood, like the oil hidden in the sesame seed, it (the *Hamsa*, the soul) dwells in the deepest depth of us: to know that is to free oneself from death."

Hamsa means "swan"

Hamsa (*Hong-Sau*) is also a scriptural name for the Supreme Lord. It is a *bij* mantra, or seed mantra, and is to be found in the most ancient *Rig Veda*.

In the *Rig-Veda*, the *Hamsa* was depicted as a bird of light. In meditation, that noble white bird spreads its vibratory wings and carries us to the luminous heavens of consciousness.

Parama-hamsa or *Param-hansa* means "supreme swan" and is the highest spiritual title in India, given to yogis whose consciousness is equally at home on earth and in heaven. Yogananda wrote his title as *Paramhansa*. It could also be translated as the "supreme I-am-He."

Hong-Sau could justifiably be described as the soul's "natural mantra," because deep within us, on a subtle level, our breath is constantly affirming, day, and night, without ever ceasing: "*Hong-Sau, Hong-Sau*, I am He, I am Spirit."

The scope of the *Hong-Sau* technique

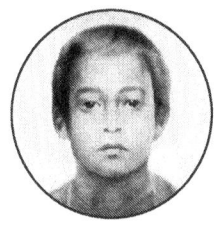

"Mukunda," Yogananda as a child

The *Hong-Sau* technique is not intended to remain hidden, accessible only to a few select seekers. It is a treasure for *everyone*, for all cultures, all religions, all types of persons, and all ages: it is, as Yogananda points out, "universally applicable."

Yogananda himself practiced it intensely even as a child: "As a boy, I used to practice *Hong-Sau* sometimes for seven hours at a time, until I entered the breathless state of ecstasy."*

His teachings give it great importance. He told a disciple: "If you want to be a Master in this lifetime, then, along with your other meditation practices, practice *Hong-Sau* at least two hours a day."†

---

* *The Essence of Self-Realization*. Chapter 18, quote 22.
† *The Essence of Self-Realization*. Chapter 13, quote 5.

Do not be alarmed! For beginners, 15 to 30 minutes are sufficient. Enjoyment is the key for deciding how long to meditate. A good piece of advice to remember is that in meditation, *quality* is more important than *quantity*.

The inner solution

Yogananda described *Hong-Sau* as the "highest technique of concentration."

Where do we concentrate? The answer of the yogis, from time immemorial, has always been: *within ourselves*, because nowhere else can we find the peace and joy that we are seeking.

The outer world keeps promising us that joy and yet is unable to keep its promise for long. It behaves like a beautiful cloud which appears glorious in the sky. We love it as it shimmers golden in the sunset. But already the next morning that same cloud may be dark, bringing rain and making our day gray and foggy.

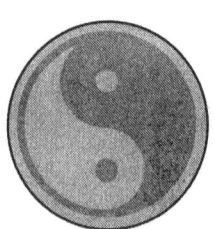

Duality is made up of opposites

Our outer life is, in fact, a constant interchange of ups and downs, in which we gain and lose, in which beauty alternates with ugliness and in which happiness and sorrow alternate exactly like the golden and gray cloud. Nothing can escape this fundamental law of outer life, which yogis call *dwaita*, or duality. It is impossible to have an *up* without its corresponding *down* and vice versa.

But we, being educated in a materialistic society, keep chasing that beautiful golden cloud, trying to grasp it, to bind it, to hold it down. The cloud smiles compassionately at our futile efforts: "Millions have tried. It will never work."

This is why the yogis have for centuries exhorted us: "Be wise. Inside alone lies your constant fulfillment, your security, and your lasting well-being."

But what do we find inside? A mass of bones, organs, and nerves? No. What yogis refer to is a subtle reality in the depth of our being wherein dwells our great Spirit, our shining soul, which is our glorious essence, forever free of gray clouds. It is joy itself. The ancient yogic tradition describes it as *Satchidananda*: ever existing, ever conscious, ever new bliss.

Yogananda exclaimed: "Ah, blindness! How long must you continue before, suffering from satiety, boredom, and disgust, you seek joy within, where alone it can be found?"*

---

* *The Essence of Self-Realization*. Chapter 1, quote 11.

Calming the waves

How can we contact our joyous essence? The method for reaching it lies in creating an inner condition of silence. This is exactly what meditation does: it methodically creates calmness, stillness, and silence. In this peaceful state we are able to perceive our true essence more clearly.

Two special aphorisms

Here are two wonderful aphorisms by Yogananda for you to contemplate. Take a minute for each one.

Yogananda

> "Silence is the altar of Spirit."

Reflect on the fact that Spirit is not to be found in any church, mosque, or synagogue, but in the temple of silence. A second and equally profound aphorism is:

> "Where movement ceases, God (Spirit) begins."

Reflect on the fact that the divine kingdom is not somewhere in a heaven up above, but within us, beginning there where all movement ceases.

These two aphorisms succinctly express the ancient definition of yoga:

> Yogas chitta vritti nirodha.

Patanjali

This means that union (*yoga*) results through the cessation (*nirodha*) of the whirlpools (*vritti*) of feeling (*chitta*). In other words, when all our inner "whirlpools" become calm and silence prevails as in meditation, our perception is deepened and is able to unite with Spirit, with our true Self.

Swami Kriyananda once put it like this: "Basically the person you are trying to please is yourself. Not your little ego, not your personality, but that higher Self, which is God. And the only God that you will ever know, at least for starters, is that higher part of your own individuality. Later you realize that it is a part of the Infinite."*

---

* In an informal talk on the anniversary of the birthday of Lahiri Mahasaya (30 September, 1995).

The *Hong-Sau* technique, therefore, provides much more than a little consolation for our troubled life: it is designed to help us discover a fulfillment which we have never felt before. It shows us how to become what Yogananda called "a smile millionaire."

May the following invocation, then, become our guiding light for this book, for every chapter that we study and for every meditation technique that we practice:

Yogananda

> *O Silent Laughter—*
> *smile Thou through my soul.*
> *Let my soul smile through my heart.*
> *And let my heart smile through my eyes.*
> *O Prince of Smiles!*
> *Be Thou enthroned*
> *beneath the canopy of my countenance,*
> *safe in the castle of my sincerity,*
> *where no rebel hypocrisy can lurk to destroy*
> *Thy presence in me.*
> *Make me a smile-millionaire,*
> *that I may scatter Thy rich smiles freely*
> *upon sad hearts everywhere!*

The method

Hong-Sau is designed to calm our restless thoughts and to concentrate our mind, helping us to enter the state of inner silence. Its effect is considerable and Yogananda makes no secret of its value: "This marvelous *Hong-Sau* exercise is one of the greatest contributions of India's spiritual science to the world."*

Why it is so particularly effective? The main reason, as the yogis explain, is that *Hong* and *Sau* are sounds which vibrate constantly within us: they are the sounds which our own breath makes on a subtle level. Yogananda, as we read above, refers to this deep reality in his *Autobiography of a Yogi*: "*Ham-sa* (pronounced *Hong-Sau*) are two sacred Sanskrit chant words possessing a vibratory connection with the incoming and outgoing breath."

* Yogoda Lessons

The Meditation of Yogananda / 8

These sounds, then, originate from deep within our being. By pronouncing them we naturally attune ourselves with our inner center, with our essence. There alone, as we said, can we become true smile-millionaires.

A gift for beginners and advanced meditators

If you are a beginner, the *Hong-Sau* technique, if practiced regularly, will naturally quiet the breath, calm the mind and interiorize your awareness. Consequently, it will perceptively increase the quality of your life on all levels, as well as your serenity, peace, and calmness. Your stress levels and tensions will diminish. You will become healthier, more balanced and centered, emotionally more stable and, in general, your life will become more enjoyable.

If you are an advanced meditator, or are trying to become one, you, too, will reap its benefits. Gradually the *Hong-Sau* technique will lead you toward breathlessness. Remember always this advanced teaching: the breath is the chord which binds our soul to the body. By stilling the breath, the soul finally becomes free. Yogananda explains that *Hong-Sau* "shows the practical method to rise above body-consciousness and realize one's self as immortal Spirit."[*]

In such advanced states of meditation, we perceive that our "immortal Spirit" is like a wave on the ocean of Spirit. This is the deepest purpose of the *Hong-Sau* technique. In fact, its literal meaning is: "I am He."

Think of a lake at night, the surface of which is not calm. It cannot reflect the beautiful moon shining in the sky. But once it becomes still, the moon's beauty is fully reflected. The same happens within us. When we sit in silence and calm our mind, we gradually perceive and "reflect" the beauty and depth of Spirit.

The structure of the book

This book is more experiential than philosophical. As Yogananda says, "Wisdom is not assimilated with the eyes, but with the atoms."[†] It is designed to help us practice, experiment, and experience the most beautiful gifts life has to offer. Each chapter will present a week of specific training. In other words, each week we will make one important step forward on the path of meditation. Every week of training is precious, rich, and deep. Readers who diligently follow the lessons in this book will experience a new level of awareness.

[*] Yogoda Lessons
[†] *Autobiography of a Yogi*

The book is divided into three parts:

PART 1 is a practical guide which offers step-by-step instruction over a period of four weeks. You will systematically learn how to meditate using the *Hong-Sau* technique. It is meant for readers who are new, or relatively new, to meditation.

The *Hong-Sau* technique itself is quite simple. Why then this slow "week-by-week" process? The reason for offering the *Hong-Sau* technique in successive steps is because such a systematic training will help you enter more effectively into your inner world. In other words: the technique is simple, but it is not so simple to practice it well. Proceeding slowly means going farther. The patient student will, in the end, attain victory.

If you already are a meditator, or know the *Hong-Sau* technique, but are not happy with the results, diligently follow the proposed four-week training and see if your experience gradually becomes more satisfying.

The scientific approach

Put the technique to the test as though you were a scientist of the inner world. Observe what happens both to your meditation and to your daily life. In your inner laboratory, examine the results of your experiments. Meditation, if done correctly, works, no matter what we believe or do not believe.

Yogananda, in fact, described meditation as "a science" and welcomed a scientific approach to both daily life and spirituality. Regarding this, he says: "In physics and chemistry, if a person wants the right answers he must ask the right questions. The same is true also in life. Try to find out why so many people are unhappy. Then, having understood that, seek the best way of achieving lasting happiness. Insist on finding practical solutions—formulas that will work for everyone. One's approach to life should be as scientific as the physicist's to his study of the universe. Religion itself should adopt a more scientific approach to life. It should seek practical solutions to life's fundamental problems. Indeed, spiritual principles offer the most universally practical solutions there are."*

The *Hong-Sau* technique works efficiently because we consciously apply the calming effect of the breath, the power of mantra (specific sounds), together with keen inner concentration. It is a "psycho-physical science and develops all-round efficiency in its students."†

* *The Essence of Self-Realization*
† Yogoda Lessons

For beginners, the book *Meditation for Starters* by Swami Kriyananda is a highly recommend supplementary text. It covers many important points such as *why* meditate, *how* to meditate, *how* to prepare for meditation and more.

Swami Kriyananda was a master teacher and a highly advanced yogi. His own life showed an inspiring yogic balance. Inwardly he was detached and immersed in bliss, while outwardly he had his feet firmly on the ground: he was a loyal friend to all, traveled around the world, enjoyed tasty food, loved inspired music, cherished beautiful art, and always appreciated good fun and laughter.

PART 2 of the book is intended for readers who already meditate and have the desire to go deeper. In a seven-week course of training, you will practice specific attitudes because for those who truly desire to attain deeper states, meditation must become a lifestyle. It is influenced by our daily attitudes, thoughts, habits, and diet.

Often, in fact, the reason why people do not succeed in going deep lies quite simply in the way they live. We cannot separate our outer life from our inner life. Figuratively speaking, we cannot put salt in our tea and then expect it to taste sweet.

The reader will be expected to apply the ancient guidelines for daily life which are expressed in Patanjali's *yama* and *niyama* (the things to do and not to do). Yogananda in fact referred to the *Yoga Sutras* of Patanjali (who is often called the father of yoga) as the "highest teaching."

For this, Swami Kriyananda's book *The Art and Science of Raja Yoga* is a highly recommended supplementary text. It is a complete yogic manual, covering all aspects of yogic living.

PART 3 is similarly divided into seven weeks of training and is designed to take us to the peak of the *Hong-Sau* technique: Self-realization, union with Spirit, expansion, bliss. On this level, our goal is to realize that our essential reality is not the physical body.

When describing the *Hong-Sau* technique, Yogananda explains: "By continued proper practice, you will feel a great calmness in you, and by and by you will realize yourself as a soul, superior to, and existing independently of, this material body."*

For this level of training, a useful supplementary text is *The Essence of Self-realization—The Wisdom of Paramhansa Yogananda*.

---

* Yogoda Lessons

Guided meditations and music

As you progress from chapter to chapter, a guided meditation or a piece of music (which you can download at: **www.crystalclarity.com/TMOY_links** will sometimes be suggested. This will make the teachings you receive more practical and enjoyable.

The Secrets of Meditation

This book is partly based on the 31 invaluable *Secrets of Meditation*,* written by Swami Kriyananda, which convey Yogananda's meditation teachings in concise form. They can be seen as tiny seeds about to sprout. Each chapter sees one of them grow into a mature tree, producing nourishing fruit for our soul.

Graphically, they appear like this:

> The **SECRET** *of* **MEDITATION** *is...*
>
> to enter instantly into
> the silence within, and not
> waste precious time in
> mental wandering.

~~~~~

Naturally, quotes from Yogananda also appear throughout the book in abundance (enough "to sink a ship," as Swami Kriyananda would say). In each chapter, the quotes are highlighted in this way:

"Don't feel badly if you find yourself too restless to meditate deeply. Calmness will come in time, if you practice regularly. Just never accept the thought that meditation is not for you. Remember, calmness is your eternal, true nature."†

---

* Also available from Crystal Clarity Publishers
† *The Essence of Self-Realization*

The inevitable challenge of meditation

The above quote raises a fundamental question: is it easy not to wander mentally in meditation? Is *Hong-Sau* a kind of magic wand which solves the eternal problem of an unruly mind? It certainly is an ancient and tested tool. Nevertheless, it would be wise not to have too many expectations, otherwise we might end up disappointed.

A more healthy and realistic expectation is to understand that meditation will always be a challenge, simply because our mind is like a monkey which jumps constantly from one place to another. We just have to accept that our mental restlessness will not disappear quickly. It is a long-term situation, which we may easily define as "normal" and "inevitable." In some of our meditations, we will be able to control the mind better, in others hardly at all.

The trick is never to become discouraged, but rather to keep going, because we keep growing *anyway*, often imperceptibly, like a child unaware that he is growing. But inevitably one day he will be fully grown.

Even Yogananda describes in his *Autobiography of a Yogi* how, just before entering into the highest state of *Cosmic Consciousness*, his mind was "distributed like leaves in a storm."

His restless experience can be of comfort to us all. If our mind wanders a lot, we shouldn't worry. All that matters is that we continue to do our best to refocus our mind, never giving up. Patience and perseverance are the quickest path toward inner growth. Also a certain amount of self-discipline is required, as it is this that helps us to go on sitting down in meditation every day.

Centuries ago meditators faced exactly the same challenge. The Indian saint Thayumanavar (1705–1744) put it humorously: "You can control a mad elephant… But control of the mind is better and more difficult."*

When you sit to meditate, every time the mind wanders, patiently bring your attention back to the *Hong-Sau* technique, even a million times. It is normal to have thoughts during meditation. The trick is to let the thoughts pass by without following and elaborating on them. Every time you return to the technique, it is a victory: you have strengthened your power of concentration.

With its profound truth, the *Autobiography of a Yogi* assures us of our final success: "*Banat, banat, ban jai,*" which freely translated means "Striving, striving, one day behold! the Divine Goal!"

* *Autobiography of a Yogi*

Meditation groups help

Joining a nearby meditation group which meets at least once a week is a great help in reaching our goal. Regular meditation by yourself can be an arduous task.

Finally, if we keep practicing, the inner paradise will manifest itself. More correctly, it has always been there, because it is the essence of our being. It is *Satchidananda*: ever existing, ever conscious, ever new bliss.

Throughout the centuries the yogic Scriptures have encouraged meditators like us with these precious words of encouragement: *tat twam asi*, "you are *that!*"*

"Handle with care"

Please see the *Hong-Sau* meditation technique not as just another technique among many, but as a precious gift. It comes from great Masters and from an ancient and sacred tradition with this message attached: "Handle with care." Handle it with love and respect. It is a treasure of gold for your spiritual life.

The inner gold might not glimmer immediately as the process takes time and effort, but the day will come when you too with joyful heart will exclaim: "I am so grateful that I started to meditate regularly. It has possibly been the most important thing I have ever done in my life."

So take a firm decision to practice each day. Tell yourself: "Everything else can wait, but my inner search cannot wait." Of course, this does not mean that you should neglect your family, your duties, or your time with friends. But probably you can reduce *something*, maybe TV, YouTube, or Facebook to make time for meditation. Or perhaps you could get up a bit earlier.

Yogananda recommends the following times for meditation: "Between 5 and 6 am, 11 and 12 am, 5 and 6 pm, 10 and 12 pm, and 11 and 12 pm."† Similarly, Swami Kriyananda teaches that the best times for meditation are dawn, noon, sunset, and midnight.

In India they often recommend *Brahma muhurta*, "the time of God," which is the hour before sunrise. This, of course, might seem quite unrealistic to you. It is not a problem. Whatever time you chose is a good time: just do it. Be constant with meditation, unwavering, starting with 15–30 minutes a day. If nothing else works during certain days, make it just 5 minutes.

Then, after three months of regular practice, observe how you feel and notice what has happened to your life.

* Chandogya Upanishad
† Praecepta Lessons

A better world

Last but not least: meditation will be a blessing not only in your personal life, but it is also a practical solution for the tensions of the world. If enough people meditated, world-peace would naturally result. Global peace starts from within. This is why a worldwide movement has been started, in which you too can participate: "Be the change!" Go to www.Ananda.org/video/be-the-change.

Be the Change!

To be a part of this movement, you pledge a certain amount of time for daily meditation. It might be a golden opportunity for you, stimulating you to be regular in your meditations and, at the same time, contributing to a more peaceful world.

WEEK 1 OF MEDITATION TRAINING

Preparation

"Muscle recharging through will power is the Yogoda feature: mental direction of life energy to any part of the body."

Autobiography of a Yogi

Preparatory practices

During this first week, we will learn important preparatory exercises to help us to more easily begin the *Hong-Sau* technique. Such preparation is like buying the right ingredients when we want to cook a tasty meal. The cooking will be easier and the meal will be tastier.

It is difficult, for example, to get up in the morning and sit down to meditate without falling asleep or thinking about all the things we have to do during the day. Equally difficult is meditating in the evening, right after work. It is all too easy to do nothing but think about everything that has happened to us or about how tired we are. It is necessary, therefore, to do something that prepares us for our meditation. Below are four practices recommended by Yogananda.

It is crucial when you begin to do your *sadhana* (spiritual practices) to train yourself to concentrate *only* on these practices, without thinking about anything else. Give serious consideration to this advice in order to remain fully in the present moment as you practice. Otherwise even the best technique will lead you nowhere.

The **SECRET** *of* **MEDITATION** *is...*

putting resolutely aside
every plan, every project, and
focusing on the moment.

(The world will be there still,
when you finish your meditation!)

Preparation technique 1: Energization exercises

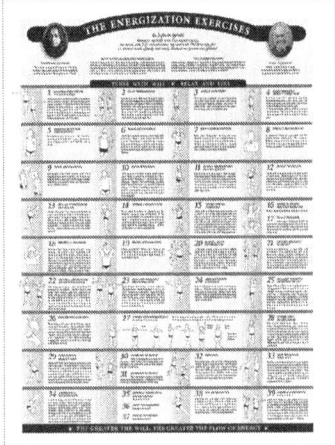

Yogananda created a set of 39 *energization exercises*, which are his original contribution to the world of yoga. These exercises were also practiced by Mahatma Gandhi, as we read in the *Autobiography of a Yogi*: "The body is visualized as divided into twenty parts; the will directs energy in turn to each section. Soon everyone was vibrating before me like a human motor. It was easy to observe the rippling effect on Gandhi's twenty body parts, at all times completely exposed to view!"

Here is how it works: our body is like a battery which can be recharged with life-force (energy, *prana*) through the direct agency of the human will. That life-force enters the body through our medulla oblongata (in the back of the neck), from where the body can be consciously and instantly recharged by an unlimited supply of cosmic energy.

The *energization exercises* teach the maximum use of will power, with which one directs life force into the muscles which are being tensed. This practice, however, not only energizes and vitalizes the muscles, but *all* tissues and cells of our body. Through the *energization exercises** we learn to "electrify" the body, healing it from within. On a spiritual level, the *energization exercises* teach us to concentrate on life force and thereby stimulate the awareness of our subtle spiritual nature. Yogananda gives us the following instructions:

"Students should remember that the Yogoda [*energization*] exercises are all to be done *slowly* at first, *gently* and *rhythmically*. Never give jerks. Every movement must be *harmonious*. If any part of the body is especially weak, send the energy *very slowly and gently*. It will be gradually strengthened. By intensity of effort you can *heal yourself very soon*, since Yogoda gives you the power to bring the only curative source, the cosmic life energy [prana], into

---

* You can follow the exercises here, led by my good friend Nayaswami Gyandev at the Ananda Village in California: www.crystalclarity.com/ee.

> contact with diseased tissues. You can feel the actual current of energy being switched on in your body, wherever you want it. The vibration which you feel is not voluntary movement, it is caused by the charge of energy into the body. Do the exercises willingly and gladly."*

20 body-part recharging

Explained below is the central exercise of the *energization exercises*, the 20 *body-part recharging* in four parts. Try to practice it right before meditation and see whether it helps you to enter calmly and energetically into the inner silence. Deep concentration is necessary during these exercises if you want to experience their beneficial results.

When performing them, keep your mind on the medulla oblongata, which is the seat of life-force (energy) in the body, and imagine the energy flowing from it to the body part being tensed.

As you practice, tense each body part in a smooth and continuous flow from low, to medium, to high tension. Low signifies a small amount of energy, medium means more energy, and high means as much energy as possible. The withdrawal of energy from the muscles is called relaxation. It is also done in three stages or degrees, resulting in complete relaxation.

Bear in mind these two axioms as you practice:

1) *"The greater the will, the greater the flow of energy."*

2) *"Tense with will, relax, and feel."*

PHASE 1. Stand upright. Inhale slowly, gradually tensing the whole body (low, medium, high) to the point where it vibrates. Gaze upward at the point between the eyebrows and with concentration feel the energy flowing into the body through the medulla oblongata. Hold the tension for a few moments and consciously fill the

* Yogoda Lessons

whole body with energy. Then exhale and slowly relax (medium, low, completely), feeling the energy as it withdraws from the body parts. Always tense with will, then relax and feel.

PHASE 2. Tense and relax the following 20 body parts, one at a time. Apply the same method as described above, gradually tensing and relaxing each part, feeling the energy flowing from the medulla oblongata and filling your body consciously with energy:

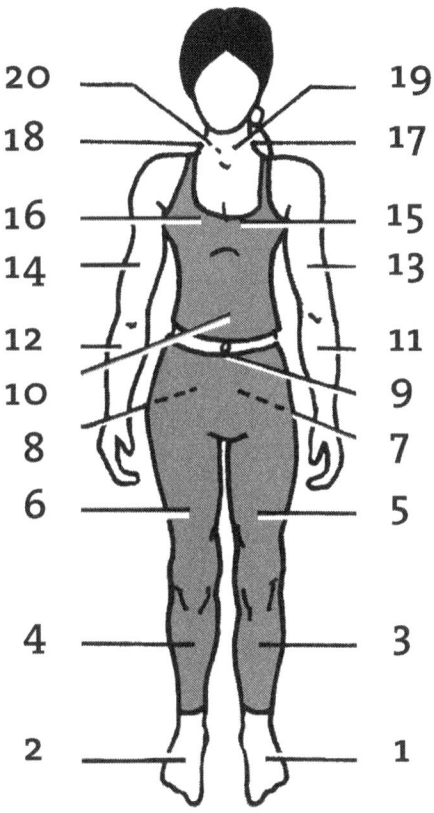

- left foot, right foot
- left calf, right calf
- left thigh, right thigh
- left buttock, right buttock
- abdomen, stomach
- left forearm, right forearm
- left upper arm, right upper arm
- left chest, right chest
- left neck, right neck
- throat, back of neck

Do not tense the neck too strongly: medium tension is sufficient.

PHASE 3. Tense (recharge) all these body-parts, one after the other, but this time maintaining medium tension in each body part. When all muscles are tensed, relax one part at a time in reverse order. In time, tense all 20 parts with one long inhalation and relax the 20 parts with one long exhalation.

PHASE 4. Repeat phase 1, but this time with the chin on the chest.

The *energization exercises* result in a sense of health, vitality, and well-being. They keep the body fit for Self-realization. Yogananda explains in his *Autobiography of a Yogi*: "The Hindu scriptures teach that the first duty of man is to keep his body in good condition; otherwise his mind is unable to remain fixed in devotional concentration."

Preparation technique 2: Asana practice

The yoga postures were recommended by Yogananda, but are optional in his teachings. For many, they work wonderfully as a preparation for meditation.

Historically, Hatha Yoga (the postures) actually had this purpose: "It is the aspirants' staircase to the heights of *Raja Yoga* (meditation)."* Ananda Yoga, the system of postures created by Swami Kriyananda, follows this original goal. He explains: "One of the main purposes of Hatha Yoga is the preparation of the body for meditation."†

You may choose simple asanas, which often actually have the best effect. Apart from preparing body and mind for a better meditative experience, they are extremely good for the health (if performed correctly), and relax the body, energizing it at the same time. Even only 15 minutes can give wonderful results (a longer time is more effective of course). For practicing Raja Yogis (meditators), 30 minutes of asana practice is enough, according to Swami Kriyananda.

According to your inner state on any given day, you may choose a different method of asana practice. In meditation, the goal is to calm (or neutralize) the vortices of our *chitta,* our inner feeling and consciousness. Yogananda explains that we can find ourselves in five states of *chitta*. Each state requires a different approach.

Ksipta State:
Restless all the time.

In this state, it might be useful to engage in a vigorous asana practice, if your body allows it. Or go running in order to sweat, or move the body vigorously in some other way.

Muddha State:
Most of the time restless and occasionally calm.

In this situation the best advice might be to practice somewhat dynamically, but allow times for calmness.

---

* *Hatha Yoga Pradipika*, first sentence.
† *The Art and Science of Raja Yoga*

Biksipta State:
Half the time calm, half the time restless.

In this case your postures can be calm and slow, with a maximum of awareness.

Ekagra State:
Most of the time calm and occasionally restless.

You might need to practice only a few asanas, holding each one for a long time. Afterwards concentrate mostly on pranayama techniques (breathing exercises).

Niruddha State:
Calm all the time and never restless.

You may not need to practice any asanas at all for your mind. You can practice them for your health.

If you have learned the asanas, during this week focus on the postures which Swami Kriyananda especially recommends as a preparation for the body for meditation; namely:

SASAMGASANA (*Hare Pose*), which gives a strong sense of compact energy, and inner control. Affirm mentally: **"I am master of my energy, I am master of myself."**

SUPTA-VAJRASANA (*Supine Firm Pose*),* in which the lower half of the body feels energetic, the upper half relaxed. Affirm: **"Energetic movement or unmoving peace: The choice is mine alone! The choice is mine!"**

End your practice with an inverted pose if you know how to practice these safely: for example **HALASANA** (*Plow Pose*), which like all inversions directs the body's energy to the brain and is therefore an excellent preparation for meditation. Affirm: **"New life, new consciousness now flood my brain!"**

---

* The asanas and the Ananda Yoga method are described in the book, *The Yoga of Yogananda*, published by Ananda Edizioni.

When you sit down to mediate, prepare your mind using the following two exercises:

Preparation technique 3: Tensing and relaxing

As you sit in meditative posture, inhale, and tense the whole body, clenching the fists. Then throw the breath out with a double exhalation, "huh, huh," and relax. Repeat three or six times. This technique helps to relax the body.

Preparation technique 4: Measured Breathing

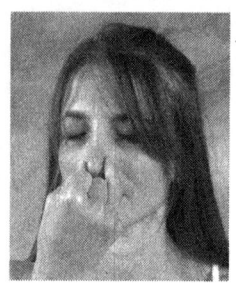

Measured Breathing has a wonderfully calming effect on the mind. It also oxygenates the body, decarbonizing it, which naturally makes you breathe less afterwards. Inhale through the nose to a count of 8, hold the breath to a count of 8, then exhale through the nose to a count of 8. Use the diaphragm. Gradually make the count longer, possibly up to 20-20-20. Whatever the count, it should always be the same for inhalation, holding, and exhalation. Repeat 6 or 12 times.

When you meditate: go "in" and "up"

After the preparatory exercises observe the natural breath, without controlling it anymore.

You will progress faster in meditation if you keep in mind where you are going: a traveler arrives more quickly if he knows his destination. Our destination in meditation is "in" and "up." If you give this conscious direction to your practice, you will arrive more quickly at your inner goal.

But what exactly do we mean by "in" and "up" in the body?

"In" refers to our subtle spine. In the yogic tradition, it is called the *sushumna*: our inner center where the chakras are located.

As you meditate and observe the breath, feel from the beginning that you are withdrawing into it: not too far back (not toward the spinal protrusions, the nodes that you feel in your back), but more toward the center of your body. That is where the subtle spine is, which Yogananda also calls "the altar of God." The Indian Scriptures describe it as *moksha marga*,* "the pathway to liberation." Jesus alluded to it: "The kingdom of God is within you."†

---

* Yoga-Yajnavalkya (IV,30)
† Luke 17: 21

"Up" refers to the spiritual eye between the eyebrows. Heaven and hell are realities within us: if our energy flows downward in the body, we say, "I feel down," "I feel low." When, on the other hand, our energy flows upward, we say that we feel "high," "in heaven." In our body, heaven is located in the spiritual eye. Yogananda describes it as the seat of Christ Consciousness, or *Kutashta Chaitanya* ("that which remains unchanged," immutable Consciousness). The Indian Scriptures describe the spiritual eye as the *trikuti* or *ajna chakra*.* Jesus also refers to it: "If therefore thine eye be single, thy whole body shall be full of light."†

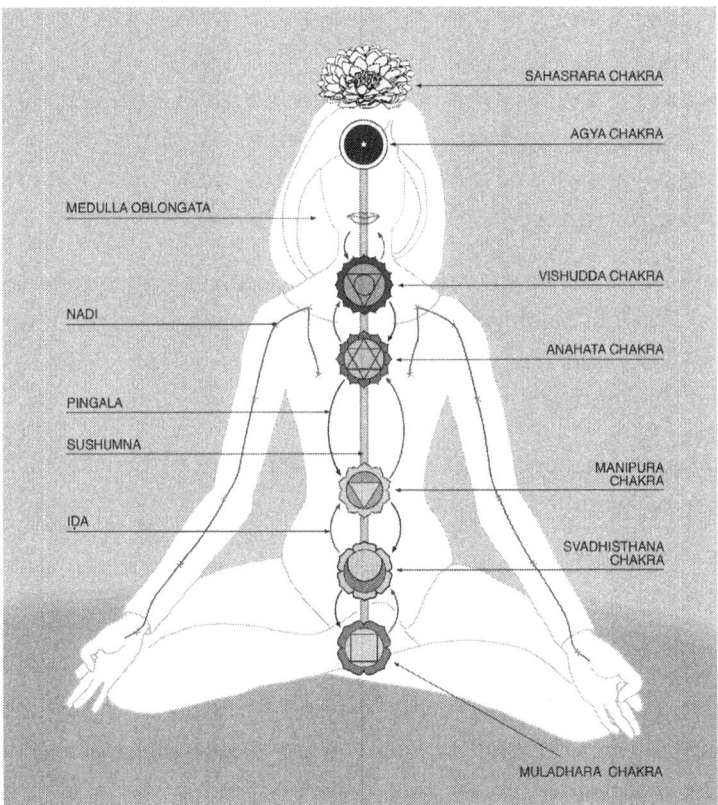

At the end of your meditation, do not observe the breath anymore or practice any technique. Simply look upward and direct your energy and consciousness toward the spiritual eye.

---

* The Bhagavad Gita (5:27, 28), for example, states: "The *muni* (one for whom liberation is the sole purpose of life) controls his senses, mind, and intellect, removing himself from contact with them by neutralizing the currents of prana and apana in the spine, which manifest (outwardly) as inhalation and exhalation in the nostrils. He fixes his gaze **in the forehead, at a point midway between the two eyebrows** (thereby converting the dual current of physical vision into the single, omniscient spiritual eye). Such a one attains complete emancipation."
† Matthew 6: 22

WEEK 1 OF TRAINING: PREPARATION EXERCISES

Follow this daily sequence each day:

1) Practice the 20 *body-part recharging* slowly and with deep attention. Focus on understanding this technique as deeply as you can, trying to feel its energizing effect. This is your most important training for this week.

2) If you have learned the asanas, practice according to your personal need. Include *Sasamgasana* (Hare Pose), *Supta-Vajrasana* (Supine Firm Pose) and *Halasana* (Plow Pose). Then relax for some time lying on your back in *Savasana* (Corpse Pose).

3) Afterwards sit up straight on a chair, cushion, or bench. Practice the tensing and relaxing exercise.

4) Follow it by the "Measured Breathing." Try the rhythm 8-8-8.

5) Keep your spine straight and watch your breath without controlling it. For now, observe it wherever it is easiest for you: in the abdomen, in the chest, or in the nose. From the very beginning, be attentive to the brief moments when the breath ceases to flow. These are precious moments of a deeper calmness. Try to take your consciousness inside.

6) During the final minutes, stop observing the breath and sit in silence, enjoying the effect of your practice. Gaze at the spiritual eye and try to transfer your awareness upward.

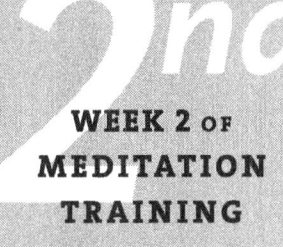

WEEK 2 OF MEDITATION TRAINING

The Body

"Overcoming restlessness of body and mind by concentration techniques has achieved astonishing results: it is no novelty at Ranchi to see an appealing little figure, aged nine or ten years, sitting for an hour or more in unbroken poise, the unwinking gaze directed to the spiritual eye."

Autobiography of a Yogi

 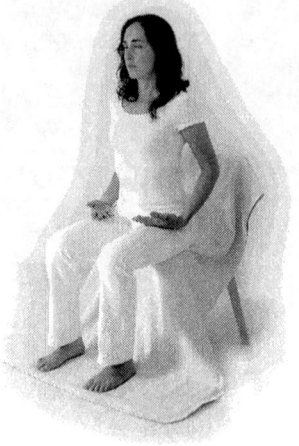 

Correct posture during meditation

After practicing the preparatory exercises, we are now ready for the next step. Our training for the second week will be the correct sitting posture, which is an extremely important factor for receiving deep inner experiences. Some readers might think that a whole week is too long for correcting just the body. This is simply not true. Don't rush, don't skip this week. A good posture is the solid foundation for the house of meditation. It will prove invaluable.

Even though correct posture is the first thing a beginner to meditation learns, alas, it often turns out that even after years of regular practice, this important foundation of his "house of meditation" is poorly constructed and still requires some important "cement," or "repair work." Because of its weak foundation—an incorrect posture—his "house of meditation" never stands firm. It cannot add higher stories in order to rise toward the sky.

Too often, in fact, one sees people meditating with their spine bent, revealing no sign of superconsciousness, no inspired energy, no inner strength.

> ### The SECRET of MEDITATION is...
>
> sitting upright with a straight spine;
> feeling that your strength emanates
> from your spine rather than from
> the muscles of your body.

Paramhansa Yogananda offers clear instructions for the correct posture for the *Hong-Sau* technique. So let us sit, choosing a chair (which Yogananda recommended for most Westerners), a meditation bench, or a cushion. Lying down is not recommended by yogis: we too easily slip into a subconscious state.

If you are a beginner to meditation, follow these instructions precisely. If, on the other hand, you are already experienced, check whether your own posture is truly "firm." Or does your foundation actually need some "repair"?

Now, as you sit for meditation, check whether you are following all the following instructions (from the *Yogoda Lessons*).

- Face east (or north)
- Sit on a woolen or silk blanket
- Keep the spine straight
- Keep the chest out
- Keep the abdomen in*
- Keep the shoulder blades together
- Keep the chin parallel to the ground
- Rest the upturned, cup-shaped palms at the junction between the abdomen and thighs
- Keep the eyes closed or half-closed, turned up, without crossing them
- If you are sitting on a chair, don't lean against it

The body should resemble a bow: our front side is the curved side of the bow and the spine is the straight string.

Follow these instructions carefully and you will feel that your body, though relaxed, definitely expresses energy, even strength. Especially be aware of your spine (the center of our body); observe how vital it feels. Can you perceive what Swami Kriyananda means in the above statement, that "your strength emanates from your spine rather than from the muscles of your body"?

Now, just for fun, try for a moment *not* to follow Yogananda's instructions. Slump just a little. Observe how your "meditative house" immediately crumbles. This bent posture is, unfortunately, quite tempting and comfortable, more so than the straight spine which requires some effort. But ask yourself with a

---

* For some persons, keeping the abdomen in creates too much tension. Maybe for that reason Swami Kriyananda taught to relax the abdomen outward. The reader may try both ways and decide. Often different suggestions work for different people.

smile: "Could I ever rise to higher consciousness like that?" "Can I affirm in this posture that I am highly inspired?"

Remember that low energy is the death of meditation. Yogananda taught: "*Intensity* is everything: intensity of *awareness*. Superconsciousness cannot be attained by halfhearted efforts."*

Motionlessness

Apart from a straight spine, there is another essential element in the body posture: to be able to sit still, without any movement. This too is not easy, but it is essential.

Swami Kriyananda writes: "Many people meditate for years without achieving any notable results, simply because they have never trained their bodies to sit still. Until the body can be mastered, higher perceptions, so subtle that they blossom only in perfect quiet, can never be achieved."†

This is why Patanjali, the ancient father of yoga, gave definitive importance to correct posture. In his famous *Yoga Sutras* (yoga aphorisms), he outlines the eightfold path. After discussing the essential yogic attitudes—the *yamas* and *niyamas*, which will be explained later—he starts the meditative process with *asana*: it refers not to the yoga postures, but to the meditative posture. It should be *sthira sukham asanam*, meaning that our sitting posture (*asanam*) must become stable (*sthira*) and comfortable (*sukham*). Stable means motionless, firm.

Swami Kriyananda explains: "A sign of perfection in *asana* is said to be the ability to sit still, without moving a muscle, for three hours."‡ In ancient India this was called *jaya-asana* (victory in the meditative posture). Three hours, of course, is an ambitious goal. We shall start with only five minutes. It will be a battle anyway, but it is a battle we have to win.

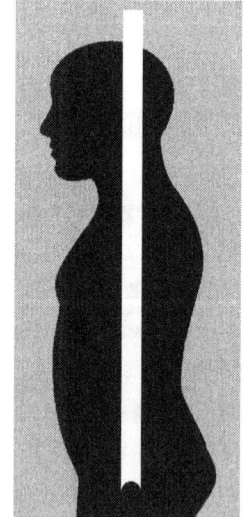

Work on this diligently. Don't move even a finger. You will soon see what difference it makes. Once you are comfortable, increase your training to ten motionless minutes. It takes discipline, of course, as the body always wants to move. But be determined to be the master in your house. Do not allow the house to control you.

---

* *The New Path*
† *The Art and Science of Raja Yoga*
‡ "Asana" today is understood as a yoga posture. In classical yoga, however, it signified a posture of meditation. The Sanskrit word *asana*, in fact, means "to sit."

Relaxation

The meditative posture, as we said, should also be *sukham*, meaning comfortable. Sitting uncomfortably makes meditation impossible. Experiment and find your perfect sitting posture. Try various cushions, benches, chairs. Relaxation is a vitally essential element. We don't want to become motionless, but stiff like a soldier. A later chapter will be dedicated to achieving deep relaxation. For now, just consider this: without physical relaxation, the mind will find it difficult to enter into deep meditation.

Swami Kriyananda expresses it like this: "Physical tensions will continue to send impulses of tension back to the brain, disturbing the very mind with which he is now trying to rid himself of mental disturbance."*

This is why the yoga asanas can be so precious.

Three methods to correct your posture:

Here are three creative methods to improve the foundation of your "house of meditation." Maybe you can think of others too.

1) The "snooze-method"

Set your alarm clock (using a pleasant, soft ringtone) on your cellphone or computer so that it rings 5 minutes after you start meditation and set the snooze option to activate after 5 minutes. Each time you hear the alarm, check your posture, asking yourself: is my spine still straight? Is my chest out? Are my shoulder blades together? Are my eyes uplifted? Do I feel that my strength is emanating from my spine? Am I motionless? Then, with as little movement possible, switch off the alarm, and in 5 minutes it will go off again.

For experienced meditators: it is a tough task to break the habit of moving the body all the time. It is equally hard to break the habit of a bent spine once it has become normal during meditation. If you have that habit, you would do well to take a step backward in your meditation: humbly concentrate not on some subtle inner realm, but on establishing a solid posture. It might even be advisable to meditate *less*, because during longer meditations we easily slip back into our old habit of a bent spine.

---

* *The Art and Science of Raja Yoga*

Here is an encouraging promise: changing that bad habit will bless you with a new meditative birth. It will bring a new tomorrow to your meditations.

2) The "film method"

Film yourself as you meditate (with your smartphone for example). When you watch it later, it may confirm that your spine is indeed straight and your body is motionless. Or you may be surprised to see that you only thought it was. In that case, don't despair. Just roll up your sleeves and start the necessary "foundation-work."

You might find encouragement and inspiration in these words by Yogananda*:

> "A bent spine is the enemy of Self-realization. Your mind is on the bent spine; you will be muscle-bound, and your electric currents will be busy with the muscles and flesh, and you cannot concentrate upon God. Practice this discipline over the body and your mind will be free to lift your consciousness from the body to the Infinite."

3) The "Master-method"

If you feel close to Yogananda or any other meditation Master, before meditation contemplate before a photo of him which shows him sitting in meditation. Absorb the great inner strength he expresses. Emulate that strength in your own meditation, in your own posture. As you meditate, try to feel that same power in your spine, while you remain relaxed at the same time.

Yoga asanas

The yoga postures can be a great blessing for achieving a good meditative posture. For example they develop physical control as well as an important spinal awareness, which many people don't have: they think they are sitting straight, but they are not. Swami Kriyananda writes in his book, *Raja Yoga*: "The hatha yogi should train himself to be deeply aware of the spine. The majority of the yoga postures relate in some way or another to the

Swami Kriyananda

* Praecepta Lessons

development of this spinal awareness, either by stretching and irrigating the spine, or by inducing a more centered consciousness."

If you practice the asanas, this week especially use **PASCHIMOTANASANA** (*Posterior Stretching Pose*) to stretch the spine and to become more aware of it. This posture also stimulates a calming energy. Affirm mentally: **"I am safe. I am sound. All good things come to me; they give me peace!"**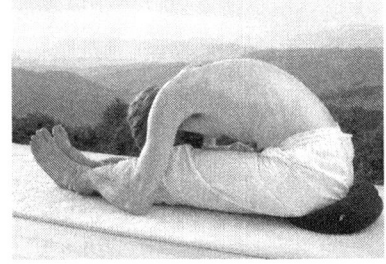

Then, for developing Kriyananda's secret of "feeling that your strength emanates from your spine," practice a backward bend, **BHUJANGASANA** (*Cobra Pose*). Try to perceive your spine very consciously, and feel that it is the spinal energy, not the muscles, which takes you into the pose and into the affirmation: **"I rise joyfully to meet each new opportunity."**

Daily Life

Practice keeping your spine straight all day long: at the dinner table, at the office desk, while walking, standing, even in the car. Create this new and noble habit. Be a yogi throughout the day. Follow this advice by Swami Kriyananda:

> "Right posture is vitally important to the yogi. A bent spine impairs the flow of energy. It also cramps the breath, making it almost impossible to breathe deeply. Right posture, however, from a standpoint of yoga, is by no means the rigid stance of a soldier on parade. One must be relaxed even while standing straight. Indeed, until one can learn to keep his spine straight he will never know how to relax perfectly. Stand in such a way that you feel yourself centered in the spine, with the rest of your body suspended from the spine in much the same way as branches are suspended from the trunk of a tree. The chest should be somewhat (but not too much) out, the shoulders a little bit back, the head neither hanging forward nor drawn back too rigidly. If you stand perfectly straight, you will find that it takes very little strength to remain standing—only enough strength to maintain your balance."*

* *The Art and Science of Raja Yoga*

WEEK 2 OF TRAINING: *STILLNESS*

Follow this sequence each day:

1) Practice the 20 *body-part recharging*.

2) Practice the postures if you know them, including *Paschimotanasana* (Posterior Stretching Pose) and *Bhujangasana* (Cobra Pose). Then relax for some time on your back.

3) Afterwards sit in a straight meditative posture. Check all the points for the correct posture outlined above.

4) Practice measured breathing to a rhythm of 10-10-10, if possible.

5) Tense and relax the body 3-6 times.

6) Then watch the breath, this time in the nostrils, without controlling it. If the mind wanders, always bring it back to the breath. Pay special attention to the moments in which the breath naturally does not flow. Enjoy these precious yogic moments. Go within.

7) In the last period of your meditation, leave the observation of the breath behind and look at the spiritual eye: raise your consciousness.

8) Let your main emphasis during this coming week be the **control over your body**: after assuming the prescribed posture, don't move. Sit straight. Check your posture often and correct it whenever necessary.

WEEK 3 OF MEDITATION TRAINING

The Mind

"*Outward longings* drive us from the Eden within; they offer false pleasures which only impersonate soul-happiness. The lost paradise is quickly regained through divine meditation."

Autobiography of a Yogi

Concentration

Now that you have a firm base—a straight and motionless body—we can go deeper: toward inner concentration, which will be the focus of our training for this coming week.

> The **SECRET** of **MEDITATION** is...
>
> one-pointed concentration;
> absorption in the peace within.

What do we one-pointedly concentrate on? The answer is: on two highly effective elements:

- The breath
- A *mantra* (sound formula).

Let's look at each of these in more detail.

Observing the breath

In meditation our goal is to concentrate inwardly. However, our mind often wanders endlessly. What should we do? Fortunately, long ago, yogis discovered a "symbiotic" relationship between the mind and the breath: a restless mind always results in a restless breath, while a calm mind produces a calm breath. The opposite is equally true: by calming the breath, we automatically calm

the mind. It is impossible to command the mind to "stop thinking," but we *can* calm the breath, which in turn will calm the mind.

A reciprocal effect begins: calming the breath calms the mind. A calmer mind in turn will slow down the breath even more, which when slower, will quiet the mind even more. The result in the end is a profound stillness of breath and mind.

How do we calm the breath? Yogis long ago devised simple, effective methods for calming it. What are these methods?

One of them is simply observing the natural flow of the breath. It works and everyone can verify it personally: just observe the natural flow of your own breath and see how automatically it becomes slower and subtler. The pauses between the breath tend to

become longer. Advanced yogis even experience periods in which the breath actually stands still for a prolonged period of time: they enter the state of natural breathlessness (called *kevala kumbhaka*). In this state, the soul is free from the body, free to expand. As we mentioned before, it is the breath which binds our soul, our consciousness, to the body.

In time, there will be longer pauses between the breaths. So, if for some time your breath naturally does not flow, enjoy that peaceful moment. Bear in mind that these times of breathlessness are our goal and are more important than the breath itself. One of the main purposes of this practice is to naturally lengthen the intervals when the breath ceases to flow.

Remember that you are not controlling the breath, but only observing it. It flows in and out by itself. In other words, we do not inhale and exhale using our will. While practicing, take the calm attitude that you are a *silent observer* of your natural breath, of which you are generally not conscious. Observe the breath, as Yogananda teaches "with greatest calmness."

The purpose of this technique is, as Yogananda explains, "conscious passivity." What does this mean? It means that, on the one hand, we are fully "conscious," alert and concentrated. But, on the other hand, we are "passive": we don't interfere, we are observers, without controlling anything. It is as if we were observing the breath of another person.

The resulting calmness enters not only our mind but also our whole body, slowing down the heart, lungs, and diaphragm.

Yogananda teaches that this physical process of calming the body during the *Hong-Sau* practice liberates a "tremendous amount" of life-force [*prana*, or energy] especially from the heart, because it has to work less. The freed life-force is then distributed all over our body, "recharging, revitalizing, and renewing all body cells, preventing their decay." It thereby "lengthens the span of life." He adds that "concentrated attention will bring a tingling sense of divine life to every body-cell."*

* Yogoda Lessons

The sacred cosmic mantra

To the observation of the breath we mentally add the ancient *Hamsa* mantra, which Yogananda taught us to pronounce as *Hong-Sau*.

In his *Autobiography*, he describes it as being "sacred," and it would therefore be wise to maintain a respectful attitude toward it. In fact, Yogananda advises us to practice *Hong-Sau* with the "greatest reverence."

Why is that? To fully appreciate the value of the *Hong-Sau* mantra, we must understand where it comes from: it has a cosmic origin. Swami Kriyananda explains it in this way: "Everything in nature is practicing the *Hong-Sau* technique. The *Hong-Sau* technique is described in the *Upanishads* as the basis of creation: the way in which God brought the universe into manifestation… The bringing of all of creation into outward manifestation, and the withdrawing of all creation back into the Spirit: these are the two breaths of *Brahman* [God], the days [creation] and nights [dissolution] of *Brahman*."*

He explains further: "The manifested universe itself might be called the respiration of Spirit: the appearance and disappearance of all things, His inhalation and exhalation… In the constant flow and ebb of nature, there is repeated endlessly, in infinite variations, the underlying truth: 'I, the manifested self, am He, the Unmanifested.' Every 'inhalation' of nature, every renewed affirmation of objective reality, becomes offered up with 'exhalation' into the Spirit, the final essence of all things. The human breath, too, flows in this continuous *mantra*. In Sanskrit the words of this *mantra*, universal to all creatures, are *Aham saha*, or, reduced to mantric words of power, *Hong-Sau*: 'I am He.'"†

As you meditate with the *Hong-Sau* technique, you may therefore visualize your breath as the breath of Spirit, the breath of *Brahman*, or the breath of the universe. Think: "It is not me breathing. It is something eternal happening and I am just a part of that eternal play."‡ Your visualization is: "The universe is breathing through me."

In other words, *Hong-Sau* is the universal breath, the cosmic mantra, which manifests in all living beings, and also within us.

---

* From a talk on the *Hong-Sau* technique.
† *The Art and Science of Raja Yoga*
‡ Swami Kriyananda, in a talk

Ajapa mantra

Our breath produces universal sounds: *Hong-Sau*. These are the sounds our own breath makes all the time. The Scripture *Shiva Sutra Vimarshini* (III. 27) explains that the mantra is constantly happening in us: "The breath is exhaled with the sound *Sa* and inhaled again with the sound *Ham*. Therefore, the individual always repeats the *Hamsa* mantra."

For this reason, the *Hamsa* mantra was known in ancient India as *ajapa mantra*, which means "unpronounced mantra," or also as *ajapa gayatri*.

One of the most respected scholars of the yogic tradition, Georg Feuerstein, describes it in his *Encyclopedic Dictionary of Yoga* in this way: "The *ajapa mantra* is the 'unpronounced mantra,' the sound *hamsa* that is continuously produced by the body as a result of the breathing process. The syllable *ham* is connected with inhalation, and *sa* with exhalation."

Another ancient Scripture, the *Vijnana Bhairava* (11b) teaches that the *Hamsa* (*Hong-Sau*) mantra is actually produced not by the body, but by our soul: "By exhaling with the sound *Sa* and inhaling with the sound *Ha*, the soul constantly repeats the *Hamsa* mantra."

Vibrational power

Hamsa (pronounced *Hong-Sau*) is the "real vedic mantra," Kriyananda stated. It is a mantra of extraordinary vibrational power and works whether we are aware or unaware of its literal meaning, as its true effectiveness lies in a highly stimulating vibration. It is in fact called *mantra-raja*, or "king of mantras" in the *Hamsa-Upanishad*.

This may be the reason why Yogananda stated that 24 hours of prayer or meditation by any other technique (except Kriya Yoga) will not produce as much spiritual advancement as one hour of *Hong-Sau* practice. Yogananda explains:

> "All sounds of the universe have a different mental effect and mental correspondence. The mental repetition of *Hong-Sau* has a great calming mental effect and helps the student in this exercise of watching the incoming and outgoing breath.*

* Yogoda Lessons

Hong-Sau: the wings of the swan

As mentioned earlier, *Hamsa* ("*Hong-Sau*") literally means swan, which is a symbol of the highest tradition of mysticism and of yoga. The swan is represented in scriptural lore as the vehicle of Brahma, the creator. This symbolism means that *Hong-Sau* is a vehicle which carries us toward Spirit.

This royal swan can be imagined to have two wings which continuously move up and down: they are the incoming and outgoing breath. When a yogi concentrates on the movements of these wings, meaning on the inflow ("*Hong*") and outflow ("*Sau*") of the breath (which, as we will see, correspond to an inner upward and downward movement in the spine), he gradually enters the natural state of stillness. The swan moves its wings less and finally stops moving them altogether: at that moment it has arrived at its destiny, the region of Spirit. There the yogi realizes: "I am He, I am Spirit, I am merged with the Divine."

Hong-Sau and *So-Ham*

There has long been a dispute in India, among scholars and yogis, regarding the two traditional mantras, which are the same, but inverted: *Hamsa* (*Hong-Sau*), meaning "I am He" and *So-Ham*, meaning "He is I." The question is not only, "which is the better mantra," but, "in our body, which sound do our inhalations and exhalations actually make?"

Dr. Mark Dyczkowski, a noted Indologist, points out in a personal letter: "In one place in the texts it says that the breath enters making the sound *ha* (i.e *ham*) and exits making the sound *sa* (*sah/so*), and in another it is the other way around." He adds yogically: "One would expect that all that is required is to *listen* carefully and we would be able to hear it just as it is. If that were the case there should be no mix up."

When Swami Kriyananda discussed the two mantras with Swami Muktananda* in India, the latter insisted on *So-ham*. Later in his life, however, Swami Muktananda too started to teach the *Hong-Sau* ("*Hamsa*") technique.

---

* Swami Muktananda (1908–1982) was one of the most famous Indian teachers of meditation in the West in the last century.

In his book, *I Am That: The Science of Hamsa in the Vijnana Bhairava*, he states that inhaling *ham* and exhaling *sa* is "the true way of practicing mantra."

Swami Kriyananda discussed the two mantras also with another great Master, Narayan Swami, who was considered to be one of the greatest scholars of his time and had a library of 150,000 books, all of which he knew. He explained that the *shastras* (Scriptures) principally teach *Hong-Sau*. Then he added the most vital point of all: "Whatever the guru says is higher than any Scripture."

In this book, we follow the teachings of Yogananda, who explained that one can legitimately reverse the *Hong-Sau* mantra to *So-Ham* ("He is I") only after Self-realization has been attained.*

Swami Kriyananda explained it further: "If you say *So-Ham*, the *Ham* means 'I,' and so the emphasis is on the 'I.' But if you think 'I am Thou' (*Hong-Sau*), then it is correct. 'You are I' (*So-Ham*) you can say *after* you have

realized Him. But when your reality is still the ego, then *So-Ham* is wrong, because it brings the energy back to the ego."†

He added that in higher stages of meditation, *So-Ham* will occur naturally: "With spiritual enlightenment, the chant *Hong-Sau* becomes transformed into the mantra *So-Ham*: 'I am He' becomes transformed into the realization 'He is I; He is my true Self.'"‡

Pronunciation of *Hong-Sau*

How to pronounce the mantra mentally? The answer is: *Hong* sounds like "song" and *Sau* like "saw."

Often it is emphasized how important it is to pronounce the Sanskrit mantras precisely and accurately. Yet there are various ways to pronounce the *Hong-Sau* mantra in India (*Hung-Sah*, etc.). Does it matter? No. "Pronounced mentally, the variations are so slight as to be virtually indistinguishable from one another, and therefore insignificant. The important thing in the practice of this technique is to deepen one's consciousness of peace, and to associate this consciousness with the repetition of the mantra. In fact, it is *one's consciousness*, truly, that determines the most correct pronunciation of any mantra."§

* *The Art and Science of Raja Yogaa*
† In an informal *satsanga* (spiritual meeting)
‡ *Awaken to Superconsciousness*
§ *The Art and Science of Raja Yoga*

For example, the famous teacher and singer Bhagavan Das (disciple of Neem Karoli Baba) exhibited the right consciousness when he practiced the mantra in India, which he pronounced as "*Ham-Sa.*" He recounts:* "A little pamphlet on the floor described a Kriya Yoga breathing technique called *Hamsa*. I inhaled '*Ham*' and exhaled '*Sa,*' visualizing the Sanskrit letters *ha* and *sa*. I had a beautiful vision of a white swan landing on a lake in the snow. These ocean-of-light experiences were very peaceful. For two weeks, all I had was mind, breath, and

tears. I sat in the lotus posture for as long as I could and kept turning within, looking at my interior world. I'd always come back to my breath, breathing in '*Ham*' and breathing out '*Sa.*' '*Hamsa*' is the natural sound the breath makes as it flows in and out. Breath becomes a curtain of energy, waving back and forth. In the middle of the curtain is a gap where eternity is experienced. I was getting these little glimpses of eternity as they came through the gap in my breath."

How to apply the *Hong-Sau* mantra during meditation

Follow Yogananda's instructions concerning the *Hong-Sau* mantra, as explained in his *Yogoda Lessons*:

"You can practice this technique anytime. Sit erect wherever you are with the spine straight, and relax. Close your eyes (or fix the gaze of your half-closed eyes in-between the eyebrows). And with the greatest calmness feel your breath as naturally going in and coming out. As the breath goes in, move the index finger of your right hand toward the thumb and mentally chant without moving your tongue '*Hong.*' As the breath goes out, move the index finger away from the thumb and mentally chant '*Sau*' (The movement of the index finger is only to differentiate inhalation from exhalation).† Do not in any way use mental willingness or force to let your breath in or out. While practicing, take the calm attitude that you are a silent observer of your natural breath coming in and going out, which you are generally not conscious of. With

---

* From his book *It's Here Now (Are You?)*, by Harmony Publishers

† The movement of the index finger is often neglected, as the usual thinking is: "I am well aware if I am inhaling or exhaling." Swami Kriyananda, however, believed that there is a deeper reason for this movement of the index finger, as there is an intimate connection between the brain and the fingers. So try to practice *Hong-Sau* with that finger movement and see if it enhances your meditation.

greatest reverence and attention practice this for at least 10 minutes. You will feel the greatest calmness in you, and by and by will realize yourself as soul, superior to and existing independently of this material body."

General advice for the *Hong-Sau* technique

- A full stomach prevents you from concentrating deeply. **Don't eat** for two hours before meditation. If that is not possible, eat only lightly.

- Face east, preferably, otherwise north, in meditation. The direction you sit affects your concentration.

- Always **meditate at the same time** if possible. It will help you concentrate.

- Create a **special place** in your home for your meditations, where you do nothing else. Make it beautiful. It will build up a vibration which helps your concentration.

- Keep meditations **short** for now: "To meditate a short time with depth is better than to meditate for long hours with the mind running wild. In the beginning, therefore, don't force yourself to sit for a long time. Strive for shorter, but deeper, meditations. Then gradually, as you become accustomed to going deep, lengthen the time you sit in meditation."*

- Remember what we said last week: keep the **body completely still**. Body and mind are connected. A motionless body makes the mind quiet.

- **Conscious enjoyment** is vital during *Hong-Sau*. Swami Kriyananda advises: "You should do the technique with the consciousness that you hope to gain from the technique... *Hong-Sau* gives the enjoyment of peace, therefore do it *with* the enjoyment

* *The Essence of Self-Realization*

of peace. Don't just do it as a mechanical exercise. Particularly concentrate on the pauses between the breaths. Don't hold the breath, but enjoy the peace that you feel when the breath isn't going. That will be your foundation, the focus from which the technique really begins to function."* So enjoy!

- It's always best to finish meditation when our enjoyment diminishes. The mind then will increasingly say, "I love to meditate." But **once a week**, try to have a longer meditation in which you expand your limits.

- If your mind wanders a lot, you may add a **visualization** to the *Hong-Sau* technique, which holds your attention better. Remember, for example, the suggestion given above: visualize the cosmic breath breathing through you. Or, alternatively, imagine the breath as a wave, flowing onto the shore, and then returning back toward the ocean. Or else imagine the passing thoughts as clouds, which you visualize moving away from your mental sky. You might also try this image of Swami Kriyananda: "The secret of meditation is… to send any vagrant thoughts in your mind soaring, like little balloons, upward through skies of Infinity until they disappear in the blue distance."

Daily Life

The *Hong-Sau* technique will gradually strengthen our concentration, like a muscle. Try to develop that concentration also during the day and the muscle will grow stronger. Do one thing at a time with full awareness. This has a wonderful effect also on our professional life as concentration is the secret of success in every undertaking.

Yoga asanas

If your choice is to practice the yoga postures, this week include **NATARAJASANA** (*The Dancing Shiva Pose*). All postures in which we balance on one leg force us to fully concentrate, otherwise we fall. Affirm: **"While I move through life, I am anchored in my Self."**

* Swami Kriyananda, from a talk on *Hong-Sau*

WEEK 3 OF TRAINING: CONCENTRATION

Follow this sequence each day:

1) Practice the 20 *body-part recharging*.

2) Should you practice the yoga postures, include *Natarajasana*.

3) Afterwards sit in a meditative posture.

4) Practice Measured Breathing: 8-8-8, or longer if possible: 12-12-12.

5) Tense and relax the whole body 3-6 times.

6) Practice Yogananda's teaching of the *Hong-Sau* mantra as described above. Observe the breath in the nostrils. Be particularly aware of the moments when the breath does not flow. Enjoy the peace these moments give you. They might become longer in time. However, don't hold the breath, only observe it.

7) Don't finish your meditation with the *Hong-Sau* technique. Use the last third or quarter of your available time to feel the effect of meditation: look upward to the spiritual eye and immerse yourself in the peace within.

8) Your specific task this week is deep concentration: every time the mind wanders, patiently return to the breath in the nostrils and to the mantra *Hong-Sau*.

WEEK 4 OF MEDITATION TRAINING

The Soul

"*The soul* is the pure, changeless image of God."

Autobiography of a Yogi

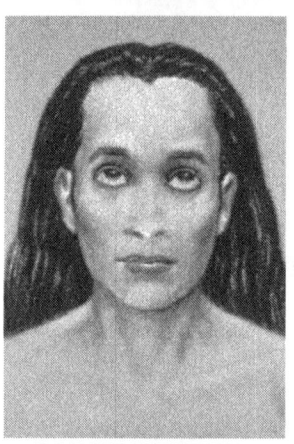

JESUS CHRIST

BABAJI-KRISHNA
Mahavatar

The soul

After concentrating for one week on preparation exercises, the second week on the body, and the third week on the mind, our focus during this fourth week will be on the soul and its qualities. However, before we turn to the soul, let's first outline the standard *Hong-Sau* technique as Yogananda taught it. Study it carefully. We will use it from now on, designating it as the "official technique."

The standard *Hong-Sau* technique

The following instructions for *Hong-Sau* are taken from Yogananda's *Praecepta Lessons* (1938). They do not include the asanas, which are an optional practice in his teachings, and are a personal choice. He does, however, write: "Long concentration must be preceded by 15 minutes practice of *Exercise 1 of the technique of rejuvenation*" (an earlier name for the *energization exercises*).

LAHIRI MAHASAYA
Yogavatar

SRI YUKTESWAR
Gyanavatar

PARAMHANSA YOGANANDA
Premavatar

The Meditation of Yogananda / 48

The complete *Hong-Sau* technique

1. Sit erect on edge of bed with feet on floor, or sit on a cushioned chair, or sit on a bed with your legs crossed, facing East, with spine straight, chest out, abdomen in, shoulder blades together, chin parallel to the ground, and up-turned, cup-shaped palms resting at the junction of the abdomen and thighs.

2. Then precede the actual practice of the *Hong-Sau* technique with an awakening prayer, which coincides with your desire or purpose of concentration; as, for example, for wisdom, peace, and contentment. Repeat the following prayer: "Heavenly Father, Jesus Christ, saints of all religions, the Spirit in my body temple, supreme master minds of India, supreme Master Babaji, great Master Lahiri Mahasaya, Master Swami Sri Yukteswar Giriji, and Guru-Preceptor, I bow to you all. Lead me from ignorance to wisdom; from restlessness to peace; from desires to contentment."

3. Inhale slowly, counting 1 to 20. Hold the breath, counting 1 to 20. Then exhale slowly, counting 1 to 20. Repeat this 6 to 12 times. Tense the whole body, clenching the fists. Relax the whole body, throwing the breath out. Repeat 6 times.

4. Then exhale quickly, and remain without breath as long as it will stay out without discomfort, and mentally wait for the breath to come in. When the breath comes in of itself, mentally say *Hong*, and when the breath goes out of itself, mentally say, *Sau*. Keep the eyes closed or open without winking or gazing, and gently fixed upward on the point between the eyebrows.

5. After practicing this technique deeply for ten minutes to one-half an hour, exhale slowly and completely. Blow all the breath out of the lungs which you possibly can, and enjoy the breathless state as long as you can without discomfort. Repeat three times. Then forget the breath and pray, or sit in silence.

For a guided Hong-Sau *practice:* www.crystalclarity.com/TMOY_links

End with a healing prayer

It would be useful to end your meditation with a healing prayer, sending energy to a person in need. First repeat a prayer which helps you to channel a higher source of energy. For example: "Divine Mother, You are omnipresent, You are in all Your children. Manifest Your healing power in this body, mind, and soul." Then rub your hands together briskly 30–60 times, energizing them. Raise the hands above the head and, with will and concentration, send a flow of energy from the medulla oblongata through the arms and hands to the person you are praying for. Feel that it is not your energy, but that you are channeling cosmic energy. Chant OM mentally as you send out the healing blessing.

The last part of the meditation

Yogananda gives special emphasis to the last part of the meditation, after practicing the *Hong-Sau* technique, when we "pray, or sit in silence."

This last part is actually the *real* meditation, while the *Hong-Sau* technique is a technique of *concentration*. Yogananda maintains that "*concentration* is the power to focus the mind on any desired line of thought. *Meditation* is that specific form of concentration which is only applied to knowing God."*

The question naturally arises: what does he mean by "God"? How can we concentrate on Him?

Fortunately, there is no religious dogma involved. You may define "God" in whatever way is meaningful to you and you are completely free to follow your own faith or definition. For atheists, it is enough that it is something greater than the ego.

The more silent we become, the better we can feel that Presence. But what exactly do we feel?

* Praecepta Lessons

Aspects of God and the soul

According to Yogananda, there are eight experiences, or qualities of Spirit and of the soul: **love, joy, peace, calmness, sound, light, wisdom, power.**

These are the qualities we should be actively looking for, especially during the last part of meditation, when we leave behind the *Hong-Sau* technique. The technique is intended to take us toward these inner experiences.

Once you feel any one of them, do not only deeply enjoy it, but try to feel that this is *who you really are*: joy, love peace, whatever you are experiencing.

> *The* **SECRET** *of* **MEDITATION** *is...*
>
> affirming that you already are
> those high truths towards which
> you aspire: inner peace,
> divine love, and perfect joy.

What to practice during the last part of meditation

After finishing the *Hong-Sau* technique, look strongly upward at the point between the eyebrows. Don't look elsewhere. Focus your gaze there. You may pray mentally and then, sitting very silent, try to intuitively feel the Divine Presence.

Swami Kriyananda puts it this way: "Never end your meditation with techniques. These are like finger exercises on the piano, which enable one to play fluently but are no substitute for actual playing. Once your mind has become focused and quiet through the practice of *Hong-Sau*, offer yourself calmly up to God."*

* *The Art and Science of Raja Yoga*

Inwardly you may pray using these words from Yogananda:

"I bow to the Spirit in the body-temple.
I bow to Thee in front and behind,
on the left and on the right,
above and beneath.
I bow to Thee everywhere,
for Thou art everywhere."

Timing

How long should this last phase of silence be? Meditation is an intuitive flow, but a good rule of thumb would be to let the last phase of meditation, after finishing with the *Hong-Sau* technique, be about a third or a quarter of your available time. For example, if you meditate for 30 minutes, it might be 7–10 minutes.

Developing intuition

During that last phase of the meditation—the phase of listening, of silence—we also develop intuition. This is a highly important process, since intuition is "the soul's power of knowing God."

Yogananda explains: "In this way, one can develop intuition: After meditation, sit still for a long time, enjoying the inner peace. As you don't cook your food and then run off without eating it, but rather, sit down and enjoy it, so also the meditation techniques help to prepare the mind, but after them, sit quietly, enjoying the 'meal' you've prepared. Many people meditate till they feel a touch of peace, but jump up then and leave their meditation for their activities. That's all right, if you have important work waiting for you, for it is always better to meditate *before* any activity, that you may feel at least *some* peace as you work. Whenever possible, however, sit for a long time after your practice of the techniques. That is when the deepest enjoyment comes. Intuition is developed by continuously deepening that enjoyment, and, later on, by holding on to its calm after-effect."*

* *Conversations with Yogananda*

Yoga asanas

If you know and practice the yoga postures, practice them in the belief that they actively express the qualities of your soul. This week give special attention to **VAJRASANA** (*Firm Pose*), which helps you tune into the *power* of the soul. Affirm: **"In stillness I touch my inner strength."**

Also practice **BALASANA** (*Child Pose*), which helps you to experience the quality of *peace* of your soul. Affirm: **"I relax from outer involvement into my inner haven of peace."**

WEEK 4 OF TRAINING: *EXPERIENCING GOD OF THE SOUL*

Follow this sequence each day:

1) Practice the 20 *body-part recharging* (pages 30–31), and—optionally—the yoga asanas.

2) Then follow the standard *Hong-Sau* technique outlined in this chapter. Go deep within, withdrawing your awareness from the outer world.

3) Let your emphasis this week be on the last phase: after *Hong-Sau*, keep your eyes raised toward the point between the eyebrows (spiritual eye). Move upward with your consciousness. **Immerse yourself in whatever perception of the soul comes to you.** Let that inner experience grow by focusing on it and by enjoying it.

Part 2 | The *Hong-Sau* Technique

Introduction to Part 2

Meditation as a Lifestyle

He laughed. "I mean [that I receive]
a pension of fathomless peace –
a reward for many years
of deep meditation.
I never crave money now.
My few material needs
are amply provided for."

Autobiography of a Yogi

The next step

This second part of the book is written mainly for those who already have a certain degree of experience with meditation. If, on the other hand, you have just started your meditation journey, it might be wiser to remain with the practices of the first part of the book for at least six months. Then you may proceed to this second part.

There is both good news and bad news for those wishing to go deeper. The good news is that the more you progress, the more fun meditation becomes. Life itself becomes more fun, happier, more fulfilled. The bad news is that nothing comes without effort. To progress, we need to invest time and energy, both in our meditations and in our outer life.

Actually, if we want to progress in meditation, what we do outside (in our daily life) is just as important as what we do inside (using techniques). As we said earlier, the way we live our life strongly influences our meditation. So are you ready to change some habits?

Deepening our practice of *Hong-Sau* by outer transformation

The crucial question is what kind of energy and consciousness do you express in your daily life? Is it compatible with the natural effects of meditation? For example, are you a relatively calm person?

It is as if you were the director of an inner "orchestra," so that during your meditation, you try to compose nice harmonies and beautiful melodies, but during the day you add too many dissonant notes and chords. When you sit down again to meditate, you notice: "My orchestra doesn't produce the melodies of the soul. The instruments are out of tune."

To "tune your inner instruments," try, when you leave your morning meditation in order to begin your daily activities, to do your best to prolong the after-effect of the *Hong-Sau* technique, whether it is a sensation of peace, harmony, joy, or whatever else you may have felt. Let it infuse your day as long as possible. Guard that feeling like a precious melody that you don't want to lose.

Later, when you meditate again, offer your day's problems into the peace of meditation. In this way, your inner and outer life begin to go hand in hand, lending support to each other.

> *The* **SECRET *of* MEDITATION** *is…*
>
> unifying your inner and your outer life:
> offering every problem up for
> resolution to the peace within;
> allowing that peace to infuse
> your outward activities.

The meditator's lifestyle

There is no way around it: deep meditation requires, at least for most people, a particular lifestyle. A highly developed yogi in the Himalayas even said: "I don't teach a single meditative technique to someone who doesn't live a sattwic (pure) lifestyle." This includes our thoughts, our reactions, our habits, our diet and our environment.

In fact, Patanjali, the father of Raja Yoga (meditation), started his eightfold path to enlightenment not with techniques, but with the yama and niyama: the ten things to do and not to do during our daily life. They are the fundamental attitudes we have to develop if we are intent on going deeper in meditation.

They are listed below together with just one reason why each yama and niyama is important for our mediation. Of course, much more could be said.

1) *Yama*: control

- *Ahimsa:* **non-violence**

Our training is to remain peaceful during the day. Thinking, feeling, or expressing violence creates mental and physical tension, which will make meditation difficult. Violent emotions agitate our nervous system. Especially anger and hate are meditation-destroyers. Try not to quarrel with anyone. Of course, we need to defend ourselves in a world where sometimes, as the Romans said, *homo homini lupus est* (man is a wolf to man). The trick is to do it without anger, hate, agitation, or violence. Non-violence also naturally takes us to a sense of union, which later on, in meditation, will make it easier to enter into deeper states.

- *Satya:* **truthfulness**

Our training is to see not only the facts, but the higher truth behind them: in people, in situations, in ourselves. Behind a negative person, in truth there shines a marvelous soul. Try to see that truth. Behind a bad situation, in truth there hides a golden opportunity. Try to discover it. Behind our own littleness, in truth there lies enormous greatness. This attitude makes it easier for us in meditation, to recognize our true nature, our Self, our soul (atman).

- *Asteya:* **non-desire**

Our training is to diminish our worldly desires as much as possible. They make us restless as they affirm: "I will be happy only when I get it." Non-desire, on the other hand, bestows peace, as it affirms: "I am content without it. My happiness lies within." Later on, in meditation, this peaceful attitude helps us to more easily find the inner pearls of joy, inspiration, love.

- *Brahmacharya:* **non-sensuality**

Our training is to not live a strongly sensuous life. Our senses according to Yogananda behave like this: "Ever fed, never satisfied; never fed ever satisfied." The strongest sensual impulse is sex, which, according to Yogananda, is one of four related forces: "In the practice of concentration, the relation between breath and life force, mind, and vital fluid (sex energy) should be known even by the spiritual beginner. A balanced control of these four bodily forces brings quick spiritual results without any downfall or hindrance."* Control of the sexual energy makes our concentration powerful during meditation.

- *Aparigraha:* **non-attachment**

Our training is to develop a sense of freedom concerning all our possessions. Attachment binds our mind and heart. Aparigraha, the attitude of freedom, will make it easier in meditation to let go of the outer world and to concentrate within. The chapter "Week 2 of Advanced Training" will be dedicated to this essential attitude.

* Praecepta Lessons

2) *Niyama*: non-control

- *Saucha:* **cleanliness, purity**

It refers to a *sattwic* (pure) lifestyle: a clean body, pure environment, pure diet, pure music, good films and books. Our training is also to develop pure thoughts, pure feelings, pure intentions, a pure character. It means constantly working on ourselves, transforming our impure aspects (which the ego often defends). All this will bring us closer in meditation to perceiving our pure Self.

- *Santosha:* **contentment**

Practicing contentment is one of the wisest things we can do. The chapter "Week 4 of Advanced Training" will be dedicated to this attitude, which has been called the "supreme virtue of the yogis." It will soon bring a sense of happy uplifting to our meditations.

- *Tapasya:* **self-control**

Our training is discipline. It is said that the highest form of tapasya is to be regular in our spiritual practices. Self-control and discipline during the day also helps to control the mind in meditation.

- *Swadhyaya:* **Self-study**

The "Week 5 of Advanced Training" and "Week 7 of Training in Self-realization" will be dedicated to two aspects of this important attitude. It will help us to more quickly perceive our true Self in meditation.

- *Ishwara Pranidhana:* **devotion**

Our training is to open our heart and direct it upward to a higher reality than the ego. This practice, too, will greatly accelerate the upliftment we can experience in meditation. A major tool for developing devotion is chanting. The chapter "Week 2 of Training in Self-realization" will be dedicated to it.

These ten *yama* and *niyama* form the first two of Patanjali's eight steps. The following six steps concern meditation. They are progressive states of evolution, like steps on a ladder. The various practices and techniques try to take us to these states.

3) Asana: posture

In this state our body sits in a meditative posture. It is perfectly still, straight, and comfortable for a prolonged time. Yoga postures and self-discipline prepare us for this state.

4) Pranayama: energy control

In this state, our energy (*prana*) has been completely withdrawn into the spine. It is achieved through various pranayama practices which control the flow of energy.

On Yogananda's path the main pranayama is Kriya Yoga, which magnetizes the spine and withdraws the life-force (energy) from the surface of the body into its inner depth, into the subtle spine, called the sushumna. It is described in Yogananda's *Autobiography of a Yogi*, and in Swami Kriyananda's *The New Path*.*

5) Pratyahara: interiorization of the mind

In this state, our mind is completely withdrawn from the outer world, from the senses. Practices like *Hong-Sau* and Kriya Yoga, and all other silent meditation techniques, are designed to take us toward this deeply inward state in which the "searchlights of the senses," to use Yogananda's description, are not turned outward toward the world anymore, but inward, toward our soul.

6) Dharana: concentration

In this state, the awareness of the meditator is fully concentrated on an inner experience which appears, such as peace, light, love, joy.

7) Dhyana: meditation

In this state, one feels not "I concentrate on peace," but "I am peace." As Yogananda put it: "Knowing, knower, known, as one."

---

* For a more detailed discussion of this topic, see Jayadev Jaerschky, *Kriya Yoga*.

> ### 8) *Samadhi*: cosmic oneness, ecstasy
> This is the supreme state. Nothing of the ego ("I am Mary") remains. Instead one experiences in deep meditation: "I am one with the universe."

Diet for Meditation

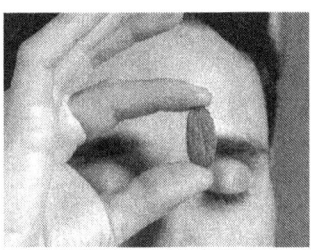

The food we eat definitely influences the quality of our meditations. Foods, yogically speaking, are classified as "heating" (agitating, making restless) or "cooling" (making us calm, or as the saying goes: "keep cool"). Swami Kriyananda explains: "Excessively spiced foods, alcoholic beverages, too many carbohydrates, artificial stimulants and stale or devitalized foods are unnatural to the body and are said to have a heating effect on it. Overcooked foods have a similar effect. Fresh fruits, nuts, raw or lightly cooked vegetables, milk or fresh milk products, and also whole grains are said to be cooling to the nervous system. Anything that excites the body is heating to it; anything that relaxes it is cooling."

For those whose desire it is to meditate deeply, he gives specific suggestions concerning diet: "Deep meditation requires a calm breath and heartbeat. It is carbon in the blood that forces them into activity. Physical exertion, tensions, and emotions feed carbon into the blood and force the lungs and heart to increase their activity. (Note, for example, how you pant after running a race.) But certain foods also have the same effect. Carbohydrates especially are to blame. The excess of carbon in the body from too many sweets forces the heart to beat faster, and the lungs to work harder. For this reason, the yogi should **not eat too many sweets**, nor **too many starches** and other **carbohydrates**. For the same reason he should avoid the use of **stimulants**, which speed up the heart. **Tea** and **coffee** are not recommended in the yoga teachings. **Overeating** can place as much of a load on the heart, however, as any stimulant. Here is the reason behind the yogic teaching, "*Stokum, stokum anekoda*" (eat a little frequently). It is well to eat more raw foods, especially fruits and nuts, and not to eat for three hours prior to any long meditation. A strong mind can force a reluctant body to do its will, but if the body is brought into harmony with one's spiritual aspirations, the resulting teamwork can be a tremendous aid on every level—physical, as well as mental and spiritual…. For the yogi, a fruit and vegetarian diet is important above all because of the calming effect it has on his mind and nervous system."

WEEK 1 OF ADVANCED TRAINING

Going Deeper with Hong-Sau

"The deeper the Self-realization of a man, the more he influences the whole universe by his subtle spiritual vibrations, and the less he himself is affected by the phenomenal flux."

Autobiography of a Yogi

Longer time for meditation

If you want to go deeper, you need to invest more time and energy in your spiritual practices (*sadhana*). This means going beyond the 15–30 minutes of daily meditation which were recommended in part 1 of this book. It might now become 45–60 minutes. The best would be to start to meditate twice a day, morning and evening. One of the two meditations can be longer. Once a week do a longer meditation, even two or three hours, if possible.

The common objection is: "But I don't have the time." This is synonymous with saying: "It is not important enough for me." If deep meditation is a priority in our life, we will find time, somehow, we will *make* time. It might also be that you meditate during your lunch break, instead of morning or evening.

{ This week }

The training for the coming week has three parts:

1) You will practice more deeply the techniques you have learnt, especially the *Hong-Sau* technique.

2) You will learn to catch "the little gold." This will be explained presently.

3) You will learn to "export" *Hong-Sau* into your daily life.

So let's start with looking at ways of deepening the various techniques.

Deepening the *energization exercises*

As you practice the 20-body-parts recharging, concentrate not only on sending the energy to the body part during tension, but also on withdrawing the energy back into the spine as you relax the muscles. This practice will also help you withdraw the energy more easily during the *Hong-Sau* technique.

Deepening the yoga asanas

If you practice the postures, try from now on to experience them mostly on an energy (*prana*) level. Prana is luminous and our energy body is a body of light. Therefore, Swami Kriyananda teaches: "It would help you to transmute the consciousness of the physicality of the human body, living in it with the thought that it is really a body of light. This is one of the functions of hatha yoga: to become aware of the body not as made of matter, but of light."*

Deeper practices of *Hong-Sau*

From now on, when you sit to meditate, begin to experiment with these advanced practices of the *Hong-Sau* technique:

1) *Hong-Sau* in the spiritual eye

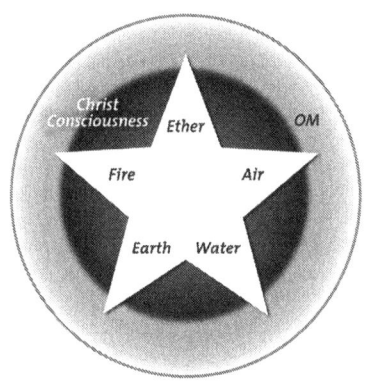

So far you have been observing the breath in the nostrils. Now gradually shift your observation of the breath higher up in the nose, until you reach the nasal cavity. In the Indian Scriptures, this is sometimes called nasikagram, which means 'the origin of the nose' (not the 'tip of the nose,' as it is often translated). The nose begins at the point between the two eyebrows, the seat of spiritual vision.

The Bhagavad Gita (6:13), for example, advises: "Holding the spine, neck, and head firmly erect and motionless, let the yogi focus his gaze at the starting point of the nose (nasikagram) between the two eyebrows; and let him not gaze elsewhere, but keep his gaze calmly one-pointed."

Yogananda further elucidates: "Concentrate on the spiritual eye; that is the door to heaven…. The single eye is right here in the forehead, and if you concentrate here, through that spiritual eye, you can see the whole universe. You will be able to see into the fourth dimension—diving into the spiritual eye, you will see infinity… Learn to control the angle of your eyes."†

During *Hong-Sau*, follow Swami Kriyananda's instructions: "Gradually, with the progressive calmness of the breath, center your awareness of it higher and higher in the nose. To raise this center of awareness, you may find it helpful if you make a special effort inwardly to relax your nose. As it becomes natural to do so, center your awareness of the breath at the point where it enters the nasal cavity. Feel it in the upper part of this passage, and visualize its movement gently fanning and awakening the Christ center in the frontal lobe of the brain."‡

---

* Excerpt from a talk entitled: "Yoga Postures as an Aid to Spiritual Growth."
† Patanjali Lessons
‡ *The Art and Science of Raja Yoga*

Elsewhere, he says: "Where should one watch the breath? Well, as the mind becomes calm, one's attention should shift to the flow of breath at the root of the nose, which is close to the seat of superconsciousness between the eyebrows, in the forehead.... To chant "Hong" at the root of the nose (at the point where the air actually enters the head, near the point between the eyebrows) brings ego-consciousness in the head gradually to its positive pole in the spiritual eye, the seat of superconscious enlightenment."*

So imagine the breath flowing in ("*Hong*") and out ("*Sau*") through the point between the eyebrows. Remember not to control the breath, just to observe it. Bring your awareness more and more into the spiritual eye, as if you were entering a temple.

Especially pay attention to and enjoy the moments in which the breath is still. In these moments, immerse yourself even more in the spiritual eye as if you were entering there the temple of God. As the pauses become prolonged, you may want to engage your attention in chanting OM mentally at the Christ center.

Hong-Sau first in the medulla oblongata

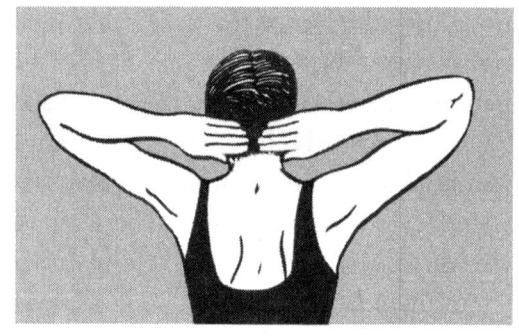

You may first practice *Hong-Sau* in the medulla oblongata for a while, before practicing it in the spiritual eye. Yogananda teaches that ego consciousness is centered in our medulla oblongata, at the base of the neck. The ego is nothing negative, but is simply the limited state of identification with the body. It can be offered into a higher identification through this technique:

> "*You may, if you like, chant Hong-Sau* first at the medulla, dissolving ego-consciousness into inner peace. After a time, as you become more interiorized, concentrate at the Spiritual Eye between the eyebrows; feel the ego only in its relationship to soul-consciousness. Indeed, concentrating at the point between the eyebrows brings the awareness closer to the upper part of the nasal passage, where the breath enters the body. To center the awareness here makes it easier to watch the breath, and at the same time bring it into harmony with spiritual awareness."†

* *Demystifying Patanjali*
† *Awaken to Superconsciousness*

2) *Hong-Sau* in the spine

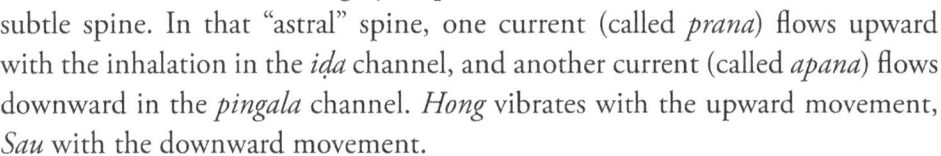

We have heard that *Hamsa* (pronounced *Hong-Sau*) is the Sanskrit word for swan. Swami Kriyananda offers a deeper explanation of this ancient mantra: "The word *Hamsa* has a further meaning. For this word also means, 'I am he' (*Aham-sa*). *Aham*, pronounced *Hong* in mantric form, becomes a *bij*, or seed, mantra, vibrating with the inhalation. Its vibration, and the movement of the breath itself, also correspond to the ascending current in the superficial spine, in the *iḍa naḍi*, or nerve channel. *Sa*, or *Sau* (my guru pronounced it to rhyme with saw), vibrates with the exhalation, and also with the descending current through the *pingala* nerve channel."*

This takes us to a deeper understanding of the *Hong-Sau* mantra: it resonates with highly important currents in our subtle spine. In that "astral" spine, one current (called *prana*) flows upward with the inhalation in the *iḍa* channel, and another current (called *apana*) flows downward in the *pingala* channel. *Hong* vibrates with the upward movement, *Sau* with the downward movement.

As the breath becomes still these two currents enter into the deep central channel, called the *sushumna*. There, in breathlessness, our soul is free from the body.

Yogananda personally taught this technique to Swami Kriyananda: "Practice watching the breath with *Hong-Sau* in the spine, if you like. Go up and down the spine with it, instead of watching its flow in the nostrils."

"Watch," the Master added, "without controlling the movement there in any way. This is an alternate practice to watching the flow of breath in the nostrils. The spine is the trunk of the 'tree of life.' God's joy is the 'sap' flowing through the trunk of the tree."† He named this technique "Baby-Kriya."

> ### The SECRET of MEDITATION is...
> visualizing your breath as a flow of energy
> in the spine, upward with inhalation,
> and downward with exhalation,
> until the flow seems a mighty river.

* *The Hindu Way of Awakening*
† *Conversations with Yogananda*

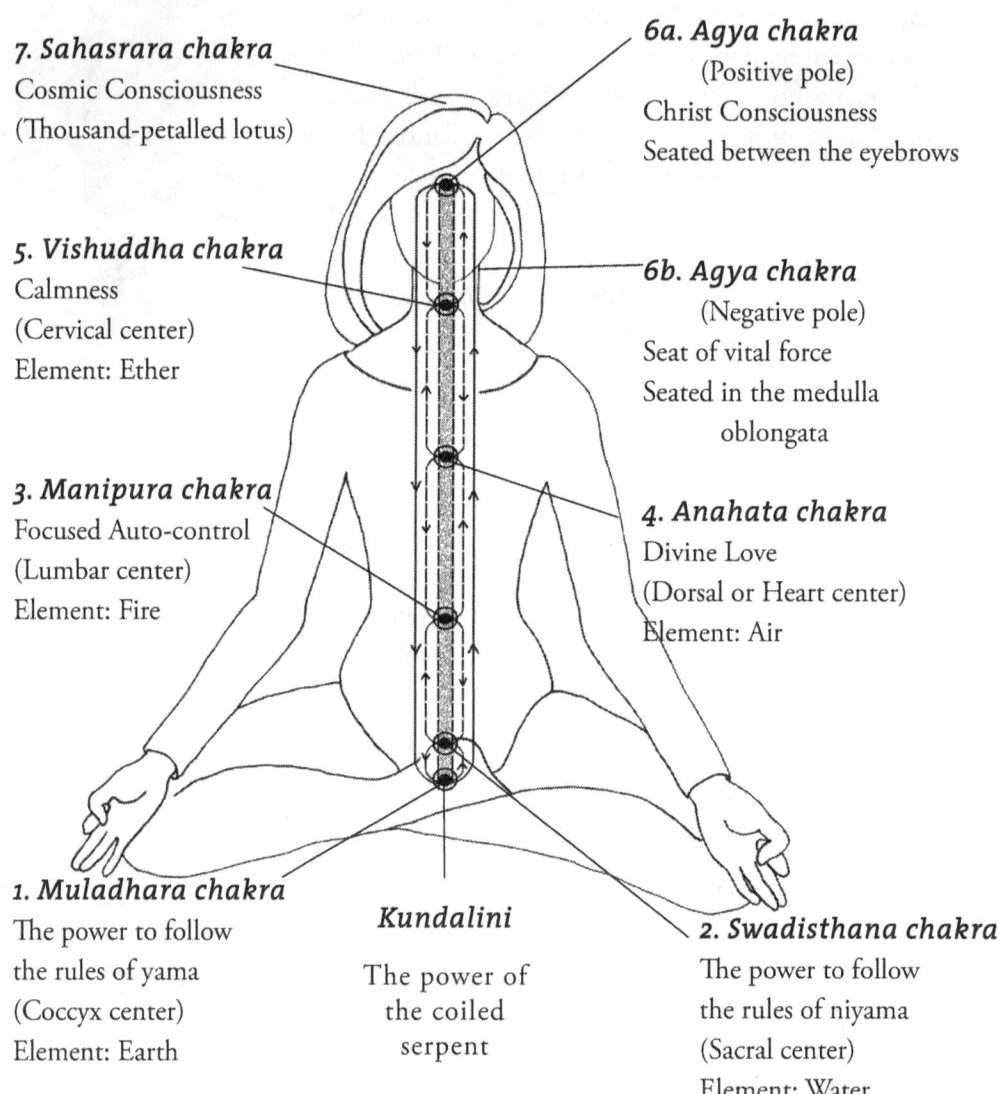

RIGHT

7. Sahasrara chakra
Cosmic Consciousness
(Thousand-petalled lotus)

5. Vishuddha chakra
Calmness
(Cervical center)
Element: Ether

3. Manipura chakra
Focused Auto-control
(Lumbar center)
Element: Fire

1. Muladhara chakra
The power to follow
the rules of yama
(Coccyx center)
Element: Earth

LEFT

6a. Agya chakra
(Positive pole)
Christ Consciousness
Seated between the eyebrows

6b. Agya chakra
(Negative pole)
Seat of vital force
Seated in the medulla
   oblongata

4. Anahata chakra
Divine Love
(Dorsal or Heart center)
Element: Air

2. Swadisthana chakra
The power to follow
the rules of niyama
(Sacral center)
Element: Water

Kundalini

The power of
the coiled
serpent

This diagram shows the nerve channels (*nadi*) and the centers (chakras) in the spine. The continuous lines indicate the movement of the energy in *ida* and *pingala*. The central channel is the sushumna; the broken lines indicate the actual course of *ida* and *pingala*.

The Meditation of Yogananda / 70

Try it. It will take you into the advanced teachings of yoga. Deep yoga happens within the spine. "The spine is the altar of God," Yogananda explained.

Here is some practical advice: when in this practice your breath becomes less, you may visualize the energy rising ("*Hong*") from the heart chakra (instead of from the base of the spine) to the spiritual eye, and then descending ("*Sau*") back to the heart; with still less breath go up and down between the medulla oblongata and spiritual eye; and with hardly any breath practice just in the spiritual eye.

The "astral breath"

It is important to understand that in the *Hong-Sau* technique, it is actually these spinal currents which produce the sounds "*Hong*" (*ham*) and "*Sau*" (*Sa*), not the physical breath. These two spinal currents—*prana* and *apana* which flow up and down in the channels *iḍa* and *pingala*—are known as the "astral breath." Swami Kriyananda writes: "As a *bij* mantra, *Hong-Sau* vibrates with the astral breath, and helps to calm the process of physical breathing."*

The Scriptures

For readers interested in historical references, this technique is not a new teaching. The ancient Scripture *Yoga Sikha Upanishad* (1.5) already reveals that the deeper practice of the *Hamsa* mantra is to be done in the astral spine: "This is chanted in the *sushumna*."

The *Yoga Chudami Upanishad* (1.30–35) explains this advanced *Hong-Sau* (*Hamsa*) practice more precisely:

> "The soul is under the control of *prana* which moves up [in *iḍa*], and moves down as *apana* [in *pingala*]. *Apana* pulls *prana*. *Prana* pulls *apana*. He who knows and realizes this mutual pull, which pulls toward the top and bottom, understands yoga. It goes outside [from kundalini] with the sound "*ha*" [the rising current in *iḍa*, connected with the inhalation], and returns inside [into kundalini, through the descending current, connected with the exhalation] with the sound "sa." The souls keep on chanting this mantra as "*Hamsa*," "*Hamsa*." The souls always keep on chanting this mantra, 20100 times during one day and night. This mantra called *ajapa gayatri* gives salvation to all yogis. Just the thought of this mantra helps one get rid of all sins. There are no

---

* *Material Success Through Yoga Principles*

practices as holy as this, no chanting equivalent to this, and no wisdom equal to this, nor shall there be in the future. This ajapa gayatri which rises from the kundalini supports the soul. This is the greatest among the sciences of the soul. He who knows this will know the Vedas."

In the light of the above description ("the *ajapa* rises from the kundalini"), also the technique described in the *Gheranda Samhita* assumes a new meaning. Usually the Sanskrit phrases *ham karena bahiri yati* ("going out it performs *ham*") and *sa karena viset punah* ("going in it performs *sa*") are understood to refer to the physical breath. But the word "breath" is never mentioned in the text, only inferred. In truth the Scriptures refer to the astral breath in the *sushumna* (deep spine), as one can see in the following sentence: it states that the mantra is to be practiced in the chakras, which are located in the *sushumna*.

Here is the text: "[The prana] goes out [of kundalini] making the sound ham, and comes back in making the sound sah, 21,600 times during a day and night. This is called ajapa gayatri which every being repeats incessantly. This ajapa japa is performed in three places: in the muladhara [root chakra],

in the anahata lotus [heart chakra], and ajna lotus [spiritual eye]." (Gheranda Samhita 5.84, 85)

When this upward and downward movement of the astral breath diminishes and finally stops, natural breathlessness (kevala kumbhaka) occurs, because, according to Yogananda, these spinal currents are the subtle cause of the physical breath.

Now we come to the second part of the training for this week...

The moment of silence: "catching the little gold"

After the *Hong-Sau* technique, when you enter into the period of silence (without *Hong-Sau*), practice "catching the little gold." By this we mean that often we don't move ahead in meditation because we passively wait for something to eventually happen. In addition, we hope for some great experience. Usually, neither one of these two expectations bring results.

It is much more effective to actively search for some *little* experience—a little peace, a little joy, a little feeling of love—and to receive this little gift with full energy and awareness. It is as if we are holding a magnifying glass in front of it. Whatever we concentrate on becomes bigger, just as when we hold a blade of grass in front of our eyes.

Swami Kriyananda explains that first we listen sensitively inside: "What, then, is meditation? Here is a good definition: Meditation is *listening*. It is listening not only with the ear, but with the *soul*—not only to sound, but to the *silent language of inspiration*."*

And whatever inspiration we feel, even if only a little, we should receive it with intense awareness and deep participation: "Meditation isn't a matter of waiting passively for something to happen. Whatever higher awareness, inspiration, or guidance you receive, participate in the experience with calm, committed awareness. For you will never attain superconsciously inspired experiences except on their own level of intense awareness."†

In short: be an intuitive Sherlock Holmes. Especially during the last phase of meditation, if you "detect" a little inspiration, receive it with intense awareness and make it grow. In this way, your small experience will expand, will become rich, fulfilling, and transforming.

What "little gold" can we expect from our *Hong-Sau* practice? Its results are manifold and unpredictable, but here are some common ones:

1) The experience of calmness

Swami Kriyananda teaches: "By concentration on the breath, the *mind becomes calmer*. This greater calmness is reflected in increasingly gentle breathing, which in turn induces still deeper concentration and calmness, a process that continues until mind and breathing both achieve perfect stillness."‡

2) The experience of interiorized energy

Yogananda explains: "This [*Hong-Sau*] technique teaches you how to switch on or off the life current [prana] from the bulb of the body (muscles, senses, heart, spine, and so forth) at will, and how to bring about perfect relaxation."§

3) The experience of the pure state of being

Swami Kriyananda speaks about this particular effect: "*Hong-Sau* leads naturally to that kind of concentration in which the will, no longer engaged busily in outward planning, is united to the intellect, and uplifted in a single, pure act of becoming."¶

**Awaken to Superconsciousness*   † Ibid   ‡ *Raja Yoga*   § Yogoda Lessons   ¶ *Raja Yoga*

In the same vein, he also sometimes explained that *Hong-Sau* can also be translated simply as "I am."

4) The experience of not feeling the body

This is an advanced perception. Yogananda writes: "This marvelous *Hong-Sau* exercise shows the practical method to rise above body-consciousness and realize oneself as immortal Spirit."*

Swami Kriyananda adds: "What I've really given you is a wonderful technique for developing concentration in meditation. The purpose of the [*Hong-Sau*] technique is, as I said, to help you to interiorize the mind. Its more fundamental purpose is to help you to rise above body-consciousness altogether, by stilling the breath."†

5) The experience of diminished breath

Yogananda teaches when discussing the *Hong-Sau* technique: "Breath is the cord that binds the soul to the body. Man lives in and requires the atmosphere of air just as a fish needs water. When he learns to rise above breath, man ascends into the celestial realms of the angels. By watching the course of the incoming and outgoing breath, the breath naturally slows down and calms the violent action of the heart, lungs, and diaphragm."‡

Swami Kriyananda adds: "Perfection in this [*Hong-Sau*] technique means to pass from breathing to breathlessness. Only in breathlessness can God be fully realized."§

6) The experience of union with God

This dimension will be discussed in Part 3 of this book. Swami Kriyananda puts it like this: "To repeat *Hong-Sau* mentally, particularly in conjunction with the breath, is to affirm again and again the truth that the little human ego is one with Brahman, the infinite Spirit: '*Hong Sau*! I am He! I am He!'"¶

---

* Yogoda Lessons † *Awaken to Superconsciousness* ‡ Yogoda Lessons § *Raja Yoga* ¶ *Ibid*

Our practice this week

To sum up: with deep awareness receive any "little gold" described above or any other inspiring experience which may come to you. Receive whatever comes fully, actively, gratefully, making it grow by concentrating on it.

How to apply *Hong-Sau* in daily life

Our third training this week is to apply the *Hong-Sau* technique in our daily life. Whenever you have a free moment, sit down and practice it for a while. Yogananda recommends: "This exercise ought to be practiced during your leisure periods, either when you are on the bus, or trolley car, or when sitting anywhere doing nothing. Just watch the breath and mentally chant *Hong-Sau* without moving the finger or closing the eyes, or fixing the gaze between the eyebrows, which might attract the attention of people around you. Just keep your eyes open without winking, looking straight ahead on some particular point. Keep the spine and head always in a straight line during the practice."*

You may even use the *Hong-Sau* technique in daily life to alleviate physical, mental, or emotional pain. It is a practice which Swami Kriyananda used: "All pain originates in the thought of ego ('Why is this happening to me?'). By mentally chanting "*Hong-Sau*" at the seat of that pain, one dissolves the ego's connection to the pain, and thereby lessens, or even dissolves, the pain itself. Try doing this while you sit in the dentist's chair… or at any other time that you experience pain, whether physically, mentally, or emotionally. Don't limit your practice to those times when you want desperately to rise above pain. Do it in response to any sensation, whether light or intense, pleasant or unpleasant, simply as an exercise in interiorization of the mind."†

Yoga asanas

If you practice the postures, during this week focus especially on **PARIGHASANA** (*Gate Pose*). Feel your body as a body of light, and direct the light (energy) upward through the spine to elevate your consciousness and experience a river of inner joy. Mentally affirm: **"Waves of joy surge upward in my spine."**

* Yogoda Lessons
† *Awaken to Superconsciousness*

WEEK 1 OF ADVANCED TRAINING:
Deeper Hong-Sau

Follow this sequence each day:

1) Practice the 20 *body-part recharging*, focusing on withdrawing the energy as you relax.

2) Optionally practice some yoga asanas, focusing on *Parighasana* (Gate Pose).

3) Then begin with the *Hong-Sau* technique. Follow the standard sequence (Week 4 of Meditation Training) but now practice **Hong-Sau in the spiritual eye or in the spine** as taught in this chapter. Always remember to pay special attention to the moments when the breath ceases to flow. Enjoy these moments of stillness.

4) In the second phase of the practice, as you learned before, focus intently on the spiritual eye without practicing any technique. Immerse yourself in your inner perception.

5) Your second training this week is to "**catch the little gold**" during meditation, as described above.

6) Your third training is to practice the *Hong-Sau* technique also in **leisure moments** during your daily life, whenever you are able to sit down quietly.

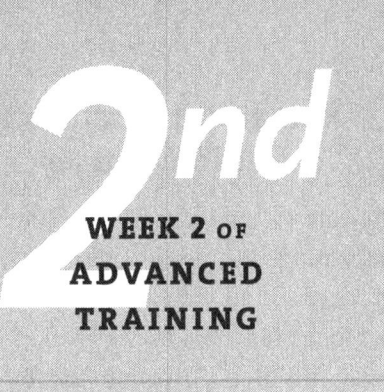

WEEK 2 OF ADVANCED TRAINING

Non-Attachment

"Attachment is blinding;
it lends an imaginary halo of attractiveness
to the object of desire."

Autobiography of a Yogi

Non-attachment brings freedom and joy

Our goal as meditators is to increase our inner joy in meditation. One important factor in attaining that joy is *aparigraha*, or non-attachment. It is one of the *yamas* and *niyamas*, taught by Patanjali, which were described earlier. So this will be our focus for the coming week.

Patanjali defined yoga itself as "calming the *vrittis* [whirlpools] of *chitta* [feeling, perception]." He points out in his Yoga Sutras (1,12): "The *vrittis* are calmed by practice and by non-attachment."

Swami Kriyananda in his little booklet *Secrets of Meditation* chose non-attachment as the very first secret, emphasizing its vital importance.

> *The* **SECRET** *of* **MEDITATION** *is...*
>
> relinquishing outward attachments,
> and affirming divine freedom within.

Why is non-attachment so essential for a deeper experience in our *Hong-Sau* practice? Imagine attachments to be like glue: they bind our mind to the outer world, blocking it from turning within during meditation.

No doubt some attachments are quite hard to "unglue," but if we work on it, we will succeed and our sense of inner freedom will grow.

Does non-attachment mean that we will love people less, love life less, love joy less? Actually, the opposite is true: we learn to love more fully, to live more fully, and to experience joy more fully. A free heart has more space to contain these treasures. Non-attachment is a joyful and liberating practice.

How should we go about practicing it?

The first step: Clarity

The first step is to get clarity about your main attachments: which things, situations, experiences, persons bind you most? Which ones engage your mind and heart most, also in meditation? Which ones are the greatest "glue" for you? Let's take some time to think about it. Write down your findings. Clearly identify your greatest attachments. Then you can work on dissolving them.

Techniques for overcoming attachments:

1) At the beginning of your meditation, before starting your *Hong-Sau* practice, visualize whatever you are attached to as being tied to your heart with a string. Then mentally take a pair of scissors and with determination cut that string. It is a happy act. Feel your heart becoming free, pure, and joyful. Affirm: "I have no need of this thing to be happy. My happiness is inside."

   Try that same exercise also with a person you are attached to. Feel, after you have cut the string, that your love hasn't diminished, but rather increased. At the same time affirm with wisdom, "Nobody is mine, nothing is mine."

   Then immediately begin your *Hong-Sau* practice and see if it naturally carries you into the inner world.

2) Again at the beginning of meditation, also try this visualization: mentally build a bonfire and throw any sensation of attachment into it. Every time you offer it into the flames, repeat the mantra Om, Swaha (meaning "OM, I offer myself"). Feel your heart becoming more and more purified, free from any lingering attachment.

3) Another possibility, again before you start with your *Hong-Sau* practice, is to repeat the following words by Swami Kriyananda, which are part of a chant entitled "I am Free." If you read music and want to learn to sing it, the notation can be found in the book *The Art and Science of Raja Yoga*.

I AM FREE

I own nothing,   In myself I am free!
I am free!   In myself I am free!
In myself   I am free, ever free!
I am free.   In myself I am free.

I own no one,   I am joyous, ever free!
I am free!   In myself I am free.
In myself   I am blissful, ever free!
I am free.   In myself I am free!

You can find the chant here:

www.crystalclarity.com/TMOY_links

4) At the end of meditation, you may affirm several times: "Nothing on earth can hold me! My soul, like a weightless balloon, soars upward through skies of eternal freedom!"*

Yoga asanas

If you practice the postures, a perfect one to develop non-attachment is **PADAHASTASANA** (*Jackknife Pose*), especially in the Ananda Yoga tradition, during which we affirm: **"Nothing on earth can hold me."**

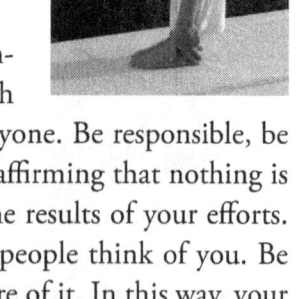

Daily life

Also practice this important "secret" of non-attachment during your daily life. Try to do everything with a joyful sense of freedom toward everything and everyone. Be responsible, be loving, do whatever you are doing *well*, while always affirming that nothing is yours forever. Practice being free inside, even from the results of your efforts. Be non-attached to praise. Be non-attached to what people think of you. Be non-attached even to your body, though take good care of it. In this way, your daily life will help your *Hong-Sau* meditation.

* *Affirmations for Self-Healing*

WEEK 2 OF ADVANCED TRAINING:
NON-ATTACHMENT

Follow this sequence each day:

1) Practice the 20 *body-part recharging*

2) Optionally practice the yoga asanas, especially focusing on *Padahastasana* (Jackknife Pose).

3) Your special training this week is this: before beginning the *Hong-Sau* technique, practice a **visualization of non-attachment** from this chapter. Vary them throughout the week and see which one works best for you.

4) Then follow the standard sequence of the *Hong-Sau* technique (Week 4 of Meditation Training), but practice *Hong-Sau* in the spiritual eye or in the spine. Go deep within.

5) The last phase of meditation is always important. Without practicing any technique, firmly look upward to the spiritual eye. Enjoy the inner upliftment and your subtle perceptions.

6) Your second training concerns daily life: **throughout the day, affirm non-attachment**, a sense of complete inner freedom.

WEEK 3 OF ADVANCED TRAINING

Relaxation

"The muscles relax during sleep, but the heart, lungs, and circulatory system are constantly at work; they get no rest. In superconsciousness, the internal organs remain in a state of suspended animation, electrified by the cosmic energy."

Autobiography of a Yogi

Learn the art of relaxation

During the coming week, we will focus on deeper relaxation, which is the key for taking our *Hong-Sau* experience to a deeper level.

Physical tensions agitate the mind. As Swami Kriyananda explains: "Most of the difficulty encountered in meditation is due to physical tension. Once tension is removed by the practice of deep relaxation, one finds meditation itself becoming increasingly enjoyable."[*]

He adds: "Relax when you meditate. Don't strain. Everything in this world is done by straining—or so it seems to the worldly mind. But meditation comes only by deeper and deeper relaxation: physical, emotional, mental, and spiritual… By perfect relaxation the whole yoga science can be mastered. This is as true for *raja yoga* as it is for *hatha yoga*, for relaxation must be taken into progressively subtle realms, through mental and emotional calmness to spiritual expansion and receptivity."[†]

> *The* **SECRET** *of* **MEDITATION** *is…*
>
> deep relaxation: Inhale, tense the body;
> throw the breath out and relax.
> Release into the surrounding atmosphere,
> like wisps of vapor, any lingering eddies
> of tension that you feel.

At first glance, this seems quite simple and straightforward advice, yet behind it lies profound yogic teaching. Yogananda defines relaxation in a way that immediately makes us realize its supreme importance for deep meditation: relaxation means the withdrawal of the life-force. He states: "The withdrawal of energy from the muscles is called relaxation. The various stages of relaxation represent the withdrawing, or dimming, of the consciousness and life current from the bulb of the body."[‡]

---

[*] *Rays of the Same Light*
[†] *The Art and Science of Raja Yoga*
[‡] Praecepta Lessons

He goes on to explain the various stages of ever-deeper relaxation which we can and must attain, if we are to "dim" our body consciousness, entering into deep soul awareness.

"Relaxation is the way to the Infinite," he states. This is teaching we should contemplate deeply in order to comprehend it.

Swami Kriyananda expresses the same thought in this way: "It might be said that conscious relaxation is the straightest path to God."*

In short: the less we are relaxed, the less our life force can flow inward and the less the inner kingdom is reachable in meditation.

In one of his *Metaphysical Meditations*, Yogananda describes relaxation as a "power." Indeed it is something to be practiced, to be strengthened gradually, almost like a muscle:

"I was a prisoner carrying a heavy load of bones and flesh, but I have broken the chains of my muscle-bound body by the power of relaxation. I am free. Now I shall try to go within."

The *20-body part* exercise used for relaxation

Alas, how chronically tensed our bodies often are! What can we do? Yogananda teaches a practical method for relaxation: lying down, one tenses and relaxes individually the 20-body parts which we have learned in the first part of this book. The emphasis and focus is on relaxation, or rather on "super-relaxation," as Yogananda calls it.

Or, alternatively, one may consciously tense the entire body, all the parts together, then relax deeply. He emphasizes: "There is no greater method of relaxation than the one you are learning. Any time you are tired or worried, tense and relax your whole body."†

Awareness plays a significant role in this technique, as Swami Kriyananda points out: "I have said that awareness is the necessary precursor of relaxation. There are many parts of the body that are tense without our conscious knowledge. How are we to become enough aware of them to relax them? The answer is, by increasing the tension throughout the body.... The best way to induce preliminary relaxation in the body is first to inhale, tense the whole body

* *Letters of Friendship*
† Praecepta Lessons

(equalizing the flow of tension throughout the body), then throw the breath out and relax the entire body at once."*

Yoga asanas

Fortunately, physical relaxation can also be greatly enhanced by correctly practicing the yoga postures. In fact, people often note how their meditation improves through asana practice. And it is small wonder given that our body in a yoga session bends forwards, backwards, sideways, twists, and also turns upside-down. As a result, physical tensions are relaxed everywhere.

At the end of an asana sequence, we lie down to experience *Savasana*, or deep relaxation. This is gold for meditators: **SAVASANA** (*Corpse Pose*) results in supreme relaxation. It is, strangely enough, quite a difficult asana. Swami Kriyananda notes: "On the surface, this would seem to be the simplest of all the poses to assume. In fact, however, because relaxation itself is so difficult, perfection in *Savasana* is rarely attained."†

Savasana helps in the development of receptivity, which is central for deep meditation. In addition, it relaxes our mind, which is equally essential. This effect is strengthened by working with the Ananda Yoga affirmation for *Savasana*: **"Bones, muscles, movement I surrender now; anxiety, elation, and depression, churning thoughts—all these I give into the hands of peace."**

However, be careful: if, as often happens, you fall asleep during *Savasana*, it has a *negative* effect on meditation. It bestows benefit only if you stay completely awake.

Mental and emotional relaxation

Of course, physical relaxation can't be separated from mental or emotional relaxation. If, during the day, we get upset, fearful, or worried, our body automatically gets tensed.

Relaxation, therefore, is life-style training. It is a central concept in yogic life: "Be even-minded and cheerful at all times," is an axiom that Yogananda emphasized. Our training is to keep our heart relaxed during the day and to relax our mind. As a consequence, our muscles too will remain relaxed. And we will take this relaxation into our *Hong-Sau* technique.

* *The Art and Science of Raja Yoga*
† *Ibid*

An inner marriage in meditation

Be careful! It's easy to be relaxed and, therefore, to slump in meditation. Let's remember to keep our relaxed body completely straight and still. "Don't move a muscle, while meditating," said the Master, "don't twitch a limb. Feel the life *inside* you, rather than your physical body, as your reality."*

The "danger" of relaxation is not only to slump, but, during meditation, to let our consciousness slips downward, into subconsciousness, into dreaming, thinking, drifting. The only remedy is high energy: practicing deep relaxation, yes, but combining it with a crystal-clear superconscious awareness.

In meditation, then, a special inner "marriage" is needed:

The "bride" is *Lady Deep Relaxation*, and the "groom" is *Lord High Energy*. Their union will result in wedded happiness for the meditator. Their "offspring" will be the soul's joy.

The deepest relaxation: the heart

These words of Yogananda serve as an invaluable guideline for attaining the deepest state of relaxation during our *Hong-Sau* practice:

"In sleep, we experience *sensory* relaxation. In death, *complete* relaxation involuntarily takes place, due to the stopping of the heart's action. If one can learn to control the heart-beat, he can experience the conscious death, leaving and re-entering the body at will; he can 'die daily', like St. Paul, and like many yogis of India, who have practiced this *Hong-Sau* exercise and have, through it, achieved mastery over the action of the heart. Such yogis have learned to leave the body voluntarily, honorably, and gladly, and are not thrown out roughly, or taken by surprise by death, when their lease on their body-temples expires.

When the heart rests, breath becomes unnecessary. The life-energy is then withdrawn from the heart and sensory nerves, and thus disconnects the telephones of the five senses, which ordinarily keep the ego perpetually disturbed and the attention scattered by incessant sensory messages from the outside world. Through sensory disconnection through *Hong-Sau*, sensations cease to arouse thoughts, which in turn cease to arouse the subconscious by associated thoughts. The attention thus becomes scientifically free from all distractions, and the student is ready to go on to advanced practice."†

* *Conversations with Yogananda*
† Praecepta Lessons

WEEK 3 OF ADVANCED TRAINING:
DEEP RELAXATION

Follow this sequence each day:

1) Practice the 20 *body-part recharging* for relaxation

2) Optionally practice the yoga asanas, especially *Savasana* (Corpse Pose).

3) Then follow the standard sequence of the *Hong-Sau* technique (Week 4 of Meditation Training), but practice *Hong-Sau* in the spiritual eye or in the spine. Take your consciousness inside.

4) Practice the second phase, without the technique, gazing upward with concentration. Move upward inwardly and absorb yourself in whatever perception comes.

5) Your special training this week is to attain **deeper relaxation than before**. Explore in your own meditation what Swami Kriyananda means by these words: "Meditation might be termed a process of *upward relaxation*, into superconsciousness."*

6) Your second training concerns your daily life: throughout the day, maintain your **heart relaxed, your thoughts relaxed, your body relaxed**.

* *Awaken to Superconsciousness*

Week 4 of Advanced Training

Contentment

"*I want nothing that is* Alexander's [the Great], for I am content with what I have, while I see that he wanders with his men over sea and land for no advantage, and is never coming to an end of his wanderings."

Autobiography of a Yogi

The supreme golden note: *santosha*

As we have seen earlier, the ten *yamas* and *niyamas* of Patanjali have, from ancient times, constituted the core attitudes for meditators. One of them—the golden one—is *santosha*, or contentment, known as the supreme virtue. It is essential for deepening our meditations.

Yogananda expresses it like this: "Work on yourself: on your reactions to outer circumstances. This is the essence of yoga: to neutralize the waves of reaction in the heart (*yogas chitta vritti nirodha*). Be ever happy inside."*

This coming week has the potential to become *surprisingly* happy, perhaps our best week ever. Why? Because, as Yogananda teaches, "circumstances are neutral." It is we who color our life from within, constantly and at every moment. And this is where our great opportunity lies.

It is as if life had given us a musical instrument so that we can play our own melody. The notes we play, however, can be somber and out of tune with our real nature, or they can be filled with beauty, harmony, and golden joy. This coming week especially, let us consciously play the golden notes of happiness.

Then, when we sit to meditate, practicing *Hong-Sau*, it will be much easier to experience the ever-new happiness of our soul.

To set the mood of *santosha* for our coming week, think of a moment when inwardly you were completely at peace, fully content with life. You didn't need anything, didn't feel the urge to go anywhere, or to do anything different from what you were doing. All agitated emotions were at rest as you fully enjoyed the moment. Concentrate on that precious mood for some time. Feel it deeply. Crystallize it within yourself.

Use this feeling as your guiding light for the coming week: it is your precious *santosha*-gold. There are two ways to consolidate it: the one outward, the other inward.

Outwardly, our task is to maintain that feeling of contentment constantly, affirming it, strengthening it day by day, no matter what may happen in our life.

Inwardly, the trick is to not wait for inner joy to appear in our meditations, but to fill them actively with contentment.

* *The Essence of Self-Realization*

> *The* **SECRET** *of* **MEDITATION** *is...*
>
> affirming contentment, rather than
> expecting God to do all the work
> of bringing you out of darkness
> into His infinite light and joy.

By training ourselves in *santosha* (conscious contentment), our inner treasure will gradually increase, turning us into a spiritual Croesus: a smile millionaire. *Santosha*, the Masters say, in time grows into a state of supreme joy. As Patanjali put it centuries ago in his *Yoga Sutras* (2.42): "Contentment leads to superlative happiness."

Isn't that an inviting prospect for our week, even more so, for our entire life?

Music

In order to infuse our consciousness directly with these ancient yogic teachings, Swami Kriyananda set them to music. A number of his songs brilliantly express *santosha*, both through their lyrics and their melody. They are great fun too.

One time a woman confronted him: "Well, *you* can write happy songs. You've never suffered!" His reply was, "It is *because* I've suffered, and learned the lesson of pain, that I've earned the right to sing happy songs! For true happiness isn't something one feels only when things are going well. The test of it is its power to transcend suffering."

May his experience become ours. Suffering afflicts us all, sometimes mercilessly so. It can make meditation impossible. However, by daily developing *santosha*, we can, through its golden power, transcend all the darkness of pain. Where there is light, darkness cannot exist.

You are invited!

A powerful way to "make the darkness flee" is to listen to joyous music. And there is great news: Swami Kriyananda is inviting us all for a special

Contentment-Concert, with his own compositions. It's a different kind of concert, however: it spans a whole week, with one song for each day. Why?

His music, Kriyananda tells us, is "philosophy in song," and so he is setting us a particular task: day by day to extract two important *santosha*-teachings from each of the songs in the concert—one for our outer life and one for our meditation. Can we do that? Let's take up the challenge. So let's gather round: a great treat is awaiting us.

---------------{ **MONDAY** }---------------

Are you ready? Well then, take your seat (mentally). Let the *Contentment-Concert* begin. Just relax into a receptive mood of listening, absorbing, and enjoying.

You can listen to the songs here: www.crystalclarity.com/TMOY_links

The first day presents us with one of Swami Kriyananda's most popular songs:

The Secret of Laughter

The secret of laughter lies in
   the laughing,
Not in the search for joy:
It's a swallow winging on the
   wind;
It's innocence in a boy.

Chorus:
Luru luru lero, luru luru lye,
Joy will come to anyone
Whose soul has learned to fly!

Joy in the singing, not in the
   song sung,
Welcome, but never crave:

If you think that laughter lies in
   things,
To things you'll be but a slave!

Joy in the giving, not in the gaining,
Grasp, and you'll never sing:
You could win the world and still be
   poor;
Win peace, and live like a king!
Sing when the sun shines, sing when
   the rain falls,
Sing when your road seems strange.
In a tempest seize the lightning flash
And ride the winds of change!

The Meditation of Yogananda / 92

To extract the *santosha*-teaching from it, we should focus on these lyrics: "It's a swallow winging on the wings, the innocence in a boy." Swami Kriyananda here teaches the concept of finding joy in little things.

Practicing it in our outer life: contentment through little pleasures

So let's accumulate the gold of contentment through little experiences. It may mean enjoying the sight of a passing bird, a laughing child or a pretty flower on the wayside. This approach is much wiser than waiting for major happy moments, which occur all too rarely in life. Swami Kriyananda explains: "Happiness is not a brilliant climax to years of grim struggle and anxiety. It is a long succession of *little* decisions simply to be happy in the moment."

Practicing it inwardly in meditation: concentrate on little experiences

Also during our meditations, instead of waiting for some grandiose experience (a special vision, an unusual phenomenon), let's attune our inner antenna to any *small* and *subtle* feeling of peace, of joy, or of depth that we might experience. Let's concentrate on these, magnifying them. In this way, our inner riches, the gold of our contentment, will increase through the magnifying power of our mind.

How advanced are you as a meditator?

Do you want to be an advanced yogi? Presumably you do, if you are reading this chapter. However, we all too easily associate progress with visions, lights, sounds, experiences, or powers. Even Yogananda as a young man had that false notion, which Sri Yukteswar had to erase from his mind: "I see that you are imagining that the possession of miraculous powers is knowledge of God. One might have the whole universe and find the Lord elusive still! Spiritual advancement is not measured by one's outward powers, but only *by the depth of his bliss in meditation.*"*

* *Autobiography of a Yogi*

It is this golden joy that then guides our daily life. Yogananda answered: "I do realize now that I have found God, for whenever the joy of meditation has returned subconsciously during my active hours, I have been subtly directed to adopt the right course in everything, even details."

So how advanced are you? To find out, take out your inner scales and weigh the gold of joy that exists in your meditations and in your daily life. The weight of that gold gives you the exact answer.

TUESDAY

Let us once again return to our *Contentment-Concert*! The second song is great fun indeed. It is, as Swami Kriyananda explained, from the "deeeeep south" (from Texas).

THE NON-BLUES

What am I doing, hanging out in this cellar?
It's like this: I'm composing a *blue*!
No, it ain't the *blues*, 'cause it's only one—
And brother, one's all I can do!

I'm hanging my head like I ought to—
(How's this? Have I got the hang of it?)
My chair is a case of gin,
And my mouth I have drooped like a Saint Bernard
Till its corners are touching my chin.

You may ask, "Why you're feeling so blue?"
Well, I ain't; I just thought I should try,
'Cause some fellow said, "All those songs of yours
Ain't for real: they don't make no one cry!"

So I thought, let's just find me some cellar,
For the only way to feel blue
Is, forget the sun and pretend the world
Is as dark as a fireplace flue.

Oh, that's realism, yeah! Love that gutter!
Yet, I wonder if we ain't been misled.
How much reality can a man see, anyway,
When he sits all day, hanging his head?

> Now, it ain't that I don't know what grief is;
> This old heart has had its full share!
> But grief's one thing, and complaining another:
> Why multiply grief with despair?
>
> For I find that this whole world around me,
> Like a mirror upon the wall,
> Smiles back when I smile, looks blue when I'm blue,
> And that blue shade I don't like at all!
>
> So I'm going back to my bad old haunts!
> My time here is almost done.
> The fact is, fellow, I can't stand this cellar;
> I just got to get out in the sun!

To extract the *santosha*-teaching from this song, let's focus on these lyrics: "For I find that this whole world around me, like a mirror upon the wall, smiles back when I smile, looks blue when I'm blue, and that blue shade I don't like at all!" Swami Kriyananda is here conveying the "mirror concept."

Practicing it in our outer life: smile at life always

Life, according to this teaching, mirrors back to us what we ourselves send out. Doesn't life give us every reason to be sad and upset, but also every reason to be happy and cheerful? Ours is the choice, each day, each moment, right here, right now. And whatever we choose will determine how life appears to us, as if we were standing in front of a mirror. As Swami Kriyananda puts it in another of his songs: "Wind on a hill sounds lonely if you're sad; free, if you're free; cheerful, if you're glad." In short: in the coming week, let us all determinedly smile at life, inviting it to smile right back at us. *Santosha* is, and always will be, the golden lifestyle.

Practicing it inwardly in meditation: affirm contentment

We all have a goldmine inside. In meditation, in our inner cave, if we develop the eyes of a gold-miner who focuses not on the gray rocks, but on any little glimmer of hidden gold, then our meditative cave will gradually shine in our eyes, revealing its riches. .

---{ **WEDNESDAY** }---

Here we are again at our Contentment-Concert. The next melody radiates with a great sense of happiness and joy. It will convey a lively Mexican atmosphere.

> **Mañana, Friends**
> Mañana, friends, the world will still be there:
> a world of suffering, a world of care.
> Today we'll dance and tell the universe,
> there's love and song for everyone.
> Fling joy, like roses, on the laughing wind,
> send melodies upon the air!
> Tell everyone that joy is theirs alone
> who smile at life and call it fair.

Swami Kriyananda is here teaching the concept of being able to set troubles aside.

Applying it in our outer life: learn to change gears

When our time comes for relaxation and rest, let's resolutely set aside all our problems, our work, difficulties, and challenges. They won't run away and will still be there afterwards for us to confront. But during our free time, let's "dance," let's have fun, be in nature, read an enjoyable book, practice lightness, increasing thereby the gold of our unshakable *santosha*.

Practicing it inwardly in meditation: avoid remaining with your problems

In meditation, too, as we all know, our mind tends to rotate around our problems and our work. Instead let's be uncompromising, resolutely putting it all aside, in order to exclusively contemplate the Divine. It's a difficult task, but it's worth it, because every effort brings a few more ounces of gold into our life.

Beat life!

Yogananda calls on us to respond to our troubles with enormous vigor: "Never let life beat you. Beat life. If you have a strong will you can overcome all difficulties."

Swami Kriyananda himself was an inspiring example of *santosha* in the midst of life's troubles and blows. He relates that in the darkest period of his life, when he was expelled from his Master's organization (SRF), he suffered immensely. Yet amazingly, all the while he perceived an undercurrent of inner joy: it was the golden glimmer of *santosha* which he had accumulated over many years though his yogic practices and right attitude. He writes: "Marvelous to relate, throughout this period, which was certainly the bleakest of my life, abandoned as I felt by God and man, I experienced, on some deep level within me, a subtle joy that never left me."*

Indeed, that inner joy never left him. In the early years of Ananda, in 1970, his first temple, which he had just constructed with a great amount of effort and investment, burnt down. Later that very day, he entered a nearby shop, singing. The proprietress exclaimed, "When our house burnt down I wept for six months! And you're *singing*!" "Why not?" Kriyananda asked. "I've lost a temple, but I haven't lost my voice."

Sing often!

Fortunately, he never lost his voice. Instead, he continued to sing always, even when his body suffered. In one memora-

* *The New Path*

ble occasion in Assisi, Italy, a few of us were at a restaurant with him. To the delight of those present, he suddenly started singing, giving an impromptu concert consisting of the funniest songs.

First he sang a hilarious American tune from the '50s: "You're the cream in my coffee, you're the salt in my stew." Naturally it gave rise to laughter from all sides. Next, he presented another amusing American song, "Alka Seltzer." For the following song, he mimicked opera, in a most dramatic way: "*O cessate di piagarmi o lasciatemi morir*" (oh stop wounding me, oh let me die). The next song was his only political song, quite funny and delightful: "Paper, Anyone?" Then he chose a love song, "John Anderson." For the finale, he performed some of his beautiful Shakespeare songs. There was joy in the air.

The moral: Whenever life becomes tough this coming week, let us respond with a song in order to "sing the blues away!" In Italy, there is a wise saying: "Sing and it will pass."

———————————————{ THURSDAY }———————————————

The next song will be pure fun, nothing more and nothing less. It conveys the colorful Hawaiian way of life.

Kriyananda admits: "The truth is, it's sheer gibberish... I have written, hmmm, something that purports to be Hawaiian, but it's not. And I even had the chutzpah to write a translation in English." When you hear him say (on the recording), "So where is the...," imagine some dressed up young dancers appearing on stage, performing a Hawaiian dance. It is golden fun, overflowing with *santosha*.

HAWAIIANA

Hali ki pa weha
Hanalei pe ha
Hakane like a na kale a kapu. :2
Ne mi Kauai ki
Wahini lei ki
Pakale hali a na pali ma.
Me luka leh i ka
Napali kane la mahini me
Hawaii le Kauai mu.

> ## "Translation"
>
> The young man sailed in a little boat from Hali,
> a distant island in the southern seas.
> He sailed in safety far, far,
> to Hanalei, the peaceful, the beautiful.
> The dark stranger, alas, was kapu (taboo).
>
> But on this isle of Kauai he met a beautiful maiden,
> who, seeing him, fell in love,
> wreathing him in a lei of fairest flowers.
>
> And so it was that this Hali man,
> wreathed in sacred flowers from the Napali coast,
> became purified of all sin,
> and united in holy love to this Napali maid.
>
> She took him home with her and wedded him,
> in the land of Hawaii, on the fair island of Kauai,
> according to the rites of the ancient land of Mu.

To extract the *santosha*-teaching, we should focus on the mood of the song: playfulness. It is especially important for those of us who tend to be a bit too serious.

Practicing it in our outer life: be playful

Putting this into practice, let's always make time for having fun and being playful (sometimes even play-fool), feeling free, creative, doing things no one has done, singing songs which no one has sung. As the lyrics of one of Swami Kriyananda's songs say: "Dare to be different, dare to be free."

Practicing it inwardly in meditation: have fun

Why not have some fun during our meditations too? A little creativity never hurts in order to keep them fresh (without ever sacrificing correct technique, of course). Would it even be possible to have fun with *Hong-Sau* in your meditations, playing with it?

Playfulness

In 1949, Yogananda appointed Kriyananda as head of the monks within his organization, SRF. Brother Turiyananda (1926–1990) shared his fond memories of that time: "I love Kriyananda. When he was here, there was such joy at Mt. Washington (the headquarters of SRF). Laughter rang through the halls." He inspired the monks, served them, but also had fun with them: one day he dyed shirts for them, in many different and happy colors. It was nothing but pure fun. Indeed, why be always serious in the name of spirituality? "Don't make too many rules. They destroy the spirit," Yogananda had advised Kriyananda.

At Ananda, the community he later founded, he always tried to maintain Yogananda's free and youthful spirit. Kriyananda even wrote: "Ananda encourages eccentricity."* Isn't that amazing? He enjoyed members who were original, as long as it came from their *origin*, not from the ego. And yes, some of them were (are?) quite eccentric. In short: if you happen to have a somewhat odd personality, don't worry. Just be merrily yourself, this week and all life long.

Jokes

What about joking, in the name of contentment? Yogananda advised: "Don't joke too much. Joking is a false stimulant. It doesn't spring from true happiness and doesn't give happiness. When you joke a lot, the mind becomes light and restless so that it can't meditate."†

"Not too much," however, doesn't mean never. The Master himself at times told a joke. Crystal Clarity published a book, *The Man Who Refused Heaven*, which focuses on his wonderful sense of humor. Kriyananda too told funny jokes (clean ones, of course), to make his audiences laugh and relax.

Here is a very short one: A wife says to her aged husband, "Darling, your teeth are just like the stars; they come out at night!"

* *Go On Alone*
† *The New Path*

{ FRIDAY }

Today we will continue with an instrumental number for our *Contentment-Concert*: a lively Romanian dance.

> **GYPSY HOEDOWN**
> (Listen on the internet.)

Practicing it in our outer life: remember the dancer in you

This lively melody conveys a special *santosha*-message for our life: "Dance more, in your spirit and with your body too! Dance through life, together with God, through all ups and downs." This teaching might be especially useful for those of us who tend to be a bit too rational. Life, Kriyananda teaches, is more like skiing, not like a game of chess. Skiing is a flow, a dance.

Practicing it in meditation: dance also inwardly

Try to bring the spirit of dance into your meditations also, following Yogananda's inspiration:

> "The waves of my song
> shall dance on Thine ocean
> of cosmic-rhythm
> and float me on billows of
> devotion to Thy shores."

{ SATURDAY }

Our *Contentment-Concert* finishes with an extract from a "*santosha*-poem" by Yogananda.

SMILE FOREVER*

Let smiles be the everlasting vehicle
in which you roam through life and death,
sorrow and pleasure, health and sickness alike.

Smile at death, for it pretends to destroy you,
who are the indestructible image of God.

Smile when trials burst upon you;
smile when the goblin of poverty stalks,
and when all hope threatens to leave you.

Let all things—fame, fortune, even life, leave you,
but hold on to the throne of your smile,
for if you can smile, no matter what happens,
then God will smile through you.

Smile when you are crying;
smile when you are laughing;
smile when you are losing, and smile when you are winning.
Smile when you are growing; smile when you are dying,
and you will die no more, for laughter is the Life of Spirit.

In the spark of a lasting smile
is the attainment of Immortal Happiness.

Practicing it in our outer life: smile forever!

Practice wearing an inner smile as you "roam through life and death, sorrow and pleasure, health and sickness alike."

Practicing it in meditation: smile in silence

Practice finding in the inner silence your unchangeable soul-smile.

* *East-West*, January 1934.

SUNDAY

Today, we will carry the effect of the *santosha*-concert with us. Our task is to listen to the music of subtle contentment everywhere, as if it were permeating the atmosphere wherever we go. Behind the chaos, behind difficulties, behind all appearances, there is a steady reality of contentment. That contentment, if we feel it, is a first glimpse of the bliss (Satchidananda) which permeates even the air we breathe.

Applause

Let's now give a big round of applause. Thank you, Swami Kriyananda, for this delightful *santosha*-concert. May it inspire you not only this week, but in all the weeks ahead, transforming your life into a happy experience and carrying you into joyful meditations.

Yoga asanas

Santosha is also the golden attitude for practicing the yoga asanas.

Kriyananda explains: "Practice the yoga postures always with a sense of *quiet enjoyment*. Feel almost as if you were smiling while you practice them. Learn the rhythm and capacities of your own body, and lead it gently on the pathway to perfection... One can advance far more rapidly in yoga if one bears in mind the teaching of great yogis, that contentment is the supreme virtue."*

If you practice the asanas, you can increase your inner gold of *santosha* with this little sequence:

First warm up for a few minutes.

1) Start with ⊃ **GARUDASANA** (*Eagle Pose*). Affirm and deeply feel: **"At the center of life's storms, I stand serene."**

---

* *The Art and Science of Raja Yoga*

2) Then enter into ⟲ **TRIKONASANA** (*Triangle Pose*), feeling throughout your body: **"Energy and joy flood my body cells. Joy descends to me."**

3) Next practice ⟳ **JANUSHIRASANA** (*Head-to-the-Knee Pose*). Permeate your consciousness with *santosha*: **"Left and right and all around—life's harmonies are mine."**

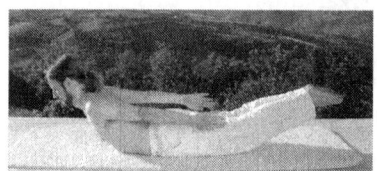

4) Follow it with ⟲ **SALABHASANA** (*Locust Pose*). Affirm and absorb: "I soar upward on wings of joy!"

5) Enter, if you can, into ⟳ **SARVANGASANA** (*Shoulderstand*). Try to feel a river of peace, joy, and harmony flowing into your head, and affirm: **"God's peace now floods my being!"** Alternatively choose any other joyful inverted pose.

6) Then enter ⓤ **SAVASANA** (*Corpse Pose*), for deep relaxation. Enjoy *santosha* for a while.

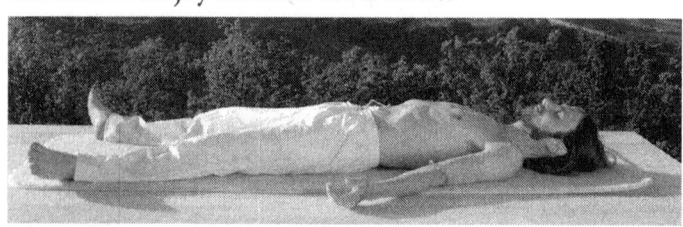

7) Finally, sit in meditation. If your body permits you, sit in ⟳ **SIDDHASANA** (*Perfect Pose*), and meditate on these words: **"I set ablaze the fire of inner joy."**

By regularly practicing this sequence with an attitude of conscious contentment, life will be obliged to mirror back to you the golden beauty of *santosha*.

The Meditation of Yogananda / 104

WEEK 4 OF ADVANCED TRAINING:
CONTENTMENT

Follow this sequence each day:

1) Practice the 20 *body-part recharging*.

2) Optionally practice the asana sequence given in this chapter.

3) Then follow the standard sequence of the *Hong-Sau* technique (Week 4 of Meditation Training), but practice *Hong-Sau* in the spiritual eye or in the spine. Withdraw your awareness within as much as you can.

4) As always, give importance to the second part of the practice, which is the real meditation: without technique look upward to the spiritual eye and concentrate on God or one of His qualities (or on your own soul qualities). Enjoy!

5) Your special training this week is to apply the teachings of the six songs of the concert. Every day (Monday to Saturday with Sunday free) listen to the message of the relative song, applying it to your practice of *santosha* (contentment) in your meditations, and during your daily life.

WEEK 5 OF ADVANCED TRAINING

Self-Analysis

"I have long exercised an honest introspection, the exquisitely painful approach to wisdom. Self-scrutiny, relentless observance of one's thoughts, is a stark and shattering experience. It pulverizes the stoutest ego. But true self-analysis mathematically operates to produce seers."

Autobiography of a Yogi

Our castle, our beauty

Imagine entering a beautiful castle (your inner depths). You admire the exquisite flowers in the gardens, the attractive furnishing and the spectacular art. Elevating music echoes through the halls. Inspiring colors meet your eyes. Everything is permeated with a peaceful and pleasing sensation. The prince himself (your soul) has brought you here and welcomes you. He now looks into your eyes and with ancient wisdom tells you:

> "Right now, you are what you are not.
> You have come here to become what you are:
> a pure soul, full of joy, riches, and beauty."

Then he adds: "You are like my princess (present state of consciousness) who yesterday fell asleep in her chambers. She had a terrible dream that she was poor and miserable. In her pain she began to cry and moan. Hearing her lament, I woke her up, reminding her who she really is."

The prince then takes you around the marvelous castle and addresses you further: "You too have accumulated many false notions about yourself, and have developed many traits which are not really yours: unwanted habits, harmful emotions, and negative thought patterns. It is time now to look at these traits. They cover up who you really are, like a black cloth covering a golden statue. Discover what these traits are so that soon you will be able to take that black cloth off. Then, and only then, can you claim your true birthright. You are in fact a noble, beautiful, and royal soul, belonging to this magnificent residence."

And so the prince sends you to his royal counselor, called *Swadhyaya* (self-study), who tells you lovingly: "This week I shall be with you, to help you. Your training will be self-analysis, which is one of Patanjali's precious *yamas* and *niyamas*."

Swami Kriyananda enters the scene to present to us this royal counselor, *Swadhyaya*. He says: "Self-study, in a yogic sense, signifies rooting out from one's heart those delusions and false attachments which prevent one from realizing who and what he really is: the Infinite Spirit. Self-study begins with the careful observation of one's thoughts, feelings, and motives. As one advances in this practice, he discovers that central reality of his being which is beyond thought, form, and substance, which cannot be observed and analyzed, which cannot even be truly defined, though it is sometimes described by its essential quality: JOY."*

Swadhyaya informs you: "If you truly want to enter into the castle of your deeper nature, and reach the advanced states of the *Hong-Sau* technique, you cannot get there but by silent meditation. You also need to analyze and transform your heart and mind in the outer life. Otherwise you will be stuck in suffering, just as the princess was in her dream. Remember Sri Yukteswar who admonished an arrogant scientist: 'I recommend an unheard-of experiment. Examine your thoughts unremittingly for twenty-four hours. Then wonder no longer at God's absence.'"†

Facing your dark spots

Swadhyaya, our wise guide to self-analysis, has some good news for us: "We don't need to kill or smother our ego. Essentially speaking, there is nothing negative in us, only positive qualities, which have been wrongly expressed. Self-analysis simply means discovering the negative traits which obscure our shining soul, and then learning how to re-channel them into something bright and positive."

Swami Kriyananda offers a few examples: "The tendency to remain set in our ways can be developed into *nishtha*, or steadfastness in our search for truth. Stolidity can become *titiksha*, or even-minded endurance in the face of life's dualities, heat and cold, pleasure and pain, joy and sorrow. Dogmatism can become *shraddha*, or true faith, born of a desire to experience truth directly, and thereby truly to know. Even heaviness of mind has its divine aspect, for it can be purified into *sthanu*, stability, or a consciousness of being always firmly centered in the Self."‡

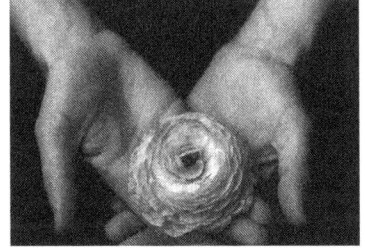

Isn't that amazing? Everything that appears as negative in our lives can be re-channeled into something positive.

Self-analysis

Yogananda too is a good friend of the royal counselor *Swadhyaya*. He recommended, for example, that we sit down at night to review the day, to analyze what we are becoming: analyzing our behavior, reactions, character, habits, strengths, and weaknesses.

* *The Art and Science Raja Yoga*   † *Autobiography of a Yogi*   ‡ *The Art and Science Raja Yoga*

In 1925 he published a Psychological Chart, which is designed to carefully analyze our character and behavior. He wrote:

"By analysis and introspection the serious spiritual student learns to know himself through this Chart, and the knowledge of how to improve will follow naturally. If one would know what he ought to be, let him first acquaint himself with what he *is*."*

In his *Yogoda Lessons*, he makes an important point:

"Self-analysis is the greatest method of progress. Without it man becomes a living machine. Every tomorrow is determined by every today. Did you ever count your faculties or measure their strength? Perhaps you do not care to think what faculties you possess or not, as long as you can earn a good living. Man is more than a civilized animal only. All his rational faculties have a deeper significance than just their use in keeping the body animal well fed, well clothed. It is necessary to maintain the body and have all the necessities of life, but there are the higher needs of the Soul, which should be fulfilled also. Suffering is the great teacher. Business failure starts the satisfied ones to think. Disease, unhappiness in family and social life makes wealthy people think. Death makes everybody think. Failure, suffering, etc., in material or spiritual life, do not occur in one's life by chance. Self-analysis tells one the nature of one's difficulties, and the knowledge of one's own power to cope with them. Self-analysis in one word furnishes us with the knowledge of what we are, what our difficulties are, what strength our faculties have, and what our mistakes or shortcomings are. Keep a mental diary every night. Consult my analytical booklet, *Psychological Chart*."

Now our royal counselor, *Swadhyaya*, hands us a list of 18 aids to self-analysis, written by Yogananda. We are asked to carefully work on each one of them and follow Yogananda's suggestion that we write our observations and analysis in a personal diary.

In addition, each evening we are asked to review our day and write down the behavior, reactions, habits, and feelings we have had.

Psychological Chart, 1925

Self-analysis homework

1) Analyze your good [*sattwic*], bad [*tamasic*] and active [*rajasic*] qualities.

2) Analyze the kind and quality of your memory.

3) Analyze the kinds and quality of your feelings, emotions, sentiments.

4) Analyze the quality of your will power.

5) Analyze your inclinations in life's business.

6) Analyze your attachments to objects of senses of touch, smell, taste, etc.

7) Analyze your predominant habits.

8) Analyze the conditions of your health and the causes that disturb it.

9) Analyze your predominant emotions of fear, anger, jealousy, etc.

10) Analyze your matrimonial or single life.

11) Analyze your instincts and hereditary tendencies.

12) Analyze your national mind and compare it with other national minds. Analyze defects and good qualities in the national mind.

13) Analyze the causes which retard progress in your business or the causes that involve it in failure.

14) Analyze the causes of your unhappiness.

15) Analyze the causes that create trouble with your wife or husband or friends.

16) Find out the methods that can make your family life better.

17) Try to find the remedy for your strong habits and inclinations which you want to get rid of.

18) Analyze your progress in contacting the Infinite.

A loving approach

Swami Kriyananda teaches us a wise and loving approach during the process of self-analysis: "Introspection means to behold oneself from a center of inner calmness, without the slightest mental bias, open to what may be wrong in oneself - not excusing it, but not condemning, either."*

Then he offers an effective affirmation:

> "I am what I am; wishing cannot change me.
> Let me therefore face my faults with gratitude,
> for only by facing them can I work on them,
> and change them."

With these words, he offers us several pearls of wisdom during our work with *Swadhyaya*, which include:

- Being fully honest while looking at our faults, without excusing them.

- At the same time never condemning ourselves. Often, in fact, when we see our "bad stuff," we feel bad, don't love ourselves anymore, or don't feel we deserve love. This is a destructive pattern which we need to eliminate very soon. The truth is that we are loved always, by God, by true Masters, by our true friends.

- "Wishing cannot change me": wishing it wasn't so won't help. Neither does looking away. The only way is to "face my faults with gratitude." Not grimly, not forcefully, but gently, with gratitude. It is an art.

- Never get discouraged in moments when you discover shortcomings. Rather, this should be a reason to celebrate. Finally you have discovered them! Finally you can work on them and get rid of them.

---

* *Affirmations for Self-Healing*

Too much and too little

Self-analysis is a balancing act. Like everything else, it can be done too much and also too little. "Too much" is when our self-analysis keeps us spinning around ourselves, around our traumas, emotions, personality. A blade of grass, when constantly held closely to the eye, appears enormous. This is what happens with "too much" self-analysis, which makes every psychological fly seem like an elephant.

"Too little" is when we resist looking at our faults with honesty. Such an attitude is usually the ego protecting its self-image, knowing instinctively that honest self-analysis will shatter that fragile image. Self-analysis reveals our weaknesses, while the ego desires confirmation, recognition, and wants to feel its value: it cries out scared, "don't touch me!"

We might all ask ourselves: Where am I, personally, in this balancing act of "too much" and "too little"? To understand, simply reflect for a moment. When someone tells you to "confront your shortcomings," what is your instinctive reaction? Do you feel an immediate sense of pleasure, thinking "great, I can analyze myself!"? Or do you feel an immediate rejection, thinking "I don't want to deal with this!"? The answer will give you a clue to which side of this balancing act you tend to be on.

The friend of *Swadhyaya*: *Saucha*

Once clarity about our strengths and our "shortcomings" has been attained, the royal counselor, *Swadhyaya*, takes us to his equally noble friend, the royal artisan called *Saucha*, or purity.

Saucha tells us: "Cleanliness applies to purity of the heart far more than to bodily cleanliness, though of course it includes the latter. Cleanliness is one of Patanjali's ten important yama and niyama."

Then he asks you: "Why do you think purity and purification play such a central role on the path of expressing your soul? Quite simply, it is because perfection is already within you. By removing your superficial 'dirt,' the truth of your innate beauty spontaneously surfaces."

He tells you a little story to illustrate his point: "Once one of our royal sculptors was asked how he was able to create such exquisite marble elephants for the palace. His answer was clear and profound: 'It is quite simple. I take a block of marble and take everything away that is not part of the perfect elephant.'"

Saucha concludes by telling us all: "You too are like that perfectly beautiful elephant, which simply needs a little more chiseling."

Yogananda expressed this thought in a devotional poem:

O Divine Sculptor, Chisel Thou my Life

Every sound that I make,
let it have the vibration of Thy voice.

Every thought that I think,
let it be saturated with the
consciousness of Thy presence.

Let every feeling that I have
glow with Thy love.

Let every act of my will be impregnated
with Thy divine vitality.

Let every thought,
every expression, every ambition,
be ornamented by Thee.

O Divine Sculptor,
chisel Thou my life
according to Thy design!*

With a pure and purified life—physically, mentally, and spiritually—the high goals of meditation are much easier to reach. In simple terms, a meditator with an angry, negative, heavy, fearful heart and mind will not get far in his meditative perceptions. Only purity can perceive Purity. Jesus said it long ago: "Blessed are the pure in heart, for they shall see God."†

The "I-am-well" method

Now you ask the royal artisan *Saucha*: "When we see an impurity or an undesirable trait in us, how can we purify and transform it?"

Saucha answers: "There are two approaches. The first one says, 'Be master of yourself; dominate this trait with a strong will, affirming it away. Tell yourself

---

* *Whispers From Eternity*
† Matthew 5:6

that you will not allow yourself to give in to this. Be victorious with an unconquerable determination.'"

The method is to affirm powerfully: "I am Master of myself," or "I am loving and kind toward others," or "I am strong in myself," or "I am calm during all storms of life," or "I am happy under all conditions," or whatever you need.

We might call this approach the *I-am-well method*. Here is how the name came about: Once Swami Kriyananda, when he lived with Yogananda, was in a bad mood. Yogananda asked him: "How are you, Walter?"* "Well..." he began. "That's good!" Yogananda interrupted. Yogananda didn't give any space to the mood, but only to the word "well."

This *I-am-well-method* works well in many cases and we need to practice it every day in a thousand circumstances. Turn on the light with a strong resolve, and the darkness will be gone as if it had never existed.

"Changing the groove" method

Saucha adds: "Then there is the second approach, for situations where we have a deep-seated tendency, of fear, let's say, or of anger, or depression, which even years of positive affirmations have not been able to eliminate."

This second approach is to look more deeply at the issue, analyzing it to find the root thought (the "groove," as Yogananda calls it) behind the emotion we are experiencing. It might be, for example, a deep-seated conviction, "I don't deserve to be happy," or "happiness makes me feel guilty."

As long as such a groove lingers with us subconsciously, we can affirm happiness all our life, but our days will still remain clouded. But once we have found that saboteur, we can install the opposite positive groove, which dispels the cloud. This is called the *changing-the-groove method*.

Positive groove techniques

Yogananda, in fact, taught powerful techniques to change such grooves instantly. One of them consists of meditating and then, while keeping the concentration fixed at the center of will between the eyebrows, of deeply affirming

---

* Yogananda used to call Swami Kriyananda "Walter," even though his name was James Donald.

the good habit that one wants to instill. And to destroy bad habits, one concentrates at the point between the eyebrows and deeply affirms that all the grooves of bad habits are being erased.

Strong spiritual healers, when they guide us in such a technique or pray for us, are able to erase harmful grooves from our brain, if we are receptive to them.

Inviting help from Above

The royal artisan *Saucha* then gives us another precious piece of advice: "Every affirmation, healing technique or effort to purify and transform ourselves becomes more powerful if we invite the help of Spirit. Pray for divine assistance. Look upward, offer yourself lovingly into Its presence and feel it fully purifying you."

> The **SECRET** *of* **MEDITATION** *is...*
>
> offering gifts of love upward from your heart to the Christ Center between the eyebrows, like the soaring flames in an all-purifying fire.

Keeping the soul-perspective

Even though we make a lot of mistakes in our lives, we should never allow them to define who we really are. "To define yourself in terms of your human limitations is a desecration of the image of God within you," Yogananda taught. "To call oneself a sinner," he added, is "the greatest sin before God." Instead he counsels us: "Never accept that bad habit as a definition of who you really are, within."*

We are all beautiful inside, forever. Isn't that something we all know instinctively?

So this week (and always!), while we are practicing *Swadhyaya* (self-analysis), let's always keep in mind the bigger picture, remembering that we are a soul and have a psychology, just as we are a soul and have a body. While we

* *The Essence of Self-Realization*

fearlessly face our shortcomings or fears, let us never forget that they are not what defines us. We are all children of the Light, forever, made in the image of God.

Yogananda puts it in the same way as *Swadhyaya* did earlier on: "If you covered a gold image with a black cloth, would you then say that the image had become black? Of course not! You would know that, behind the veil, the image was still gold. So it will be when you tear away the black veil of ignorance which now hides your soul. You will behold again the unchanging beauty of your own divine nature."*

In time you will be ready to live in the magnificent inner castle forever.

Yoga asanas

If you practice the "sacred science" (as Swami Kriyananda calls it) of the yoga postures, during this week focus on **SIMHASANA** (*Lion Pose*). Stimulate consciously the throat chakra, which contains the pure ether element. Let its pure energy radiate outward to the body, to the mind, to the heart, into your aura and actions. Affirm: **"I purify my thoughts, my speech, my every action."**

---

* *The Essence of Self-Realization*

WEEK 5 OF ADVANCED TRAINING:
SELF-ANALYSIS

Follow this sequence each day:

1) Practice the 20 *body-part recharging*.

2) Optionally pratice the yoga asanas. Focus on *Simhasana* (Lion Pose).

3) Then follow the standard sequence of the *Hong-Sau* technique (Week 4 of Meditation Training), but practice *Hong-Sau* in the spiritual eye or in the spine. Be very aware of your state of consciousness during meditation.

4) Practice the second phase, without *Hong-Sau*, looking up with deep concentration, absorbing yourself in whatever soul quality you feel.

5) Your special training this week is self-analysis: every evening, analyze how deep you were able to go, how long you meditated, which thoughts disturbed you, how the quality of your meditation was.

6) Your second training concerns daily life: again in the evening review your day, how you acted, thought, behaved, reacted. Record it in your spiritual diary.

WEEK 6 OF ADVANCED TRAINING

Radiate Blessings

"*No visitors departed* without upliftment of spirit; all knew they had received the silent blessing of a true man of God."

Autobiography of a Yogi

Radiate blessings from your heart

Usually when talking about advancing in meditation, the focus is on going *inside*. In fact, the meditative steps, as we have already seen, taught in antiquity by Patanjali (after the *yamas* and *niyamas*, the attitudes of the yogi), are:

> **Asana:** a perfectly still body.
> **Pranayama:** withdrawal of the inner energy.
> **Pratyahara:** interiorization of the senses and the mind.
> **Dharana:** concentration on an inner experience.
> **Dhyana:** oneness with that experience.
> **Samadhi:** ecstasy.

But in truth that constant *inward* movement is only one part of the equation for the sincere meditator. The other part is to be a channel of blessings radiating *outward* from you.

> *The* **SECRET** *of* **MEDITATION** *is...*
>
> radiating blessings from your heart
> outward to all the world.

Why is it important for us to radiate blessings *outward* to others, to the world? In what way is this outward flowing energy an important aspect of success in meditation?

The pitfall of the ego

The attitude of giving and "radiating blessings from your heart outward" is an important safeguard against the pitfall of the ego. Without it, all those who have a strong inward focus easily succumb to the pitfall of becoming *self*-centered instead of *Self*-centered. Once in that trough, we begin to revolve around ourselves: "*My* blessing, *my* growth, *my* happiness, *my* enlightenment, *my* problems, *my* opinion, *my* wellbeing." Spiritually speaking, our soul becomes darkened as it rests in that self-enclosed trough. If this happens, we need to launch an immediate rescue mission by "radiating blessings from our heart." Otherwise we suffer the opposite of what meditation is intended to offer us, which is *freedom* from the little ego.

Yogananda teaches: "If a devotee selfishly hoards even the grace he receives in meditation, he gives power to his ego, not to his soul."*

The ego (*ahamkara*), as he writes in his *Autobiography of a Yogi*, is "the root cause of dualism or illusion of *maya*." It means nothing less than suffering. Thinking of others, while forgetting ourselves, is a liberating practice, joyfully taking us out of the unhappy trough.

That is why it feels so good and natural for many meditators to "radiate blessings from the heart" to others. It is a practice which complements meditation, strengthening our expansion, our happiness and the smile of our soul.

The inner mountain

Our meditative life, of course, has a higher goal than simply to climb out of that trough. In truth we are climbing an inner mountain, which takes us step by step toward the sky, to the Heavens, to the Light. At whatever altitude we find ourselves on that inner mountain, one thing is certain: "Radiating blessings outward from our heart" will accelerate our journey toward the mountain-top (superconsciousness). From there we see how beautiful everything is, how connected, how eternally ONE.

If enough human beings on Earth were to climb this inner mountain of meditation, wars would end everywhere. Together, they would create a power that radiates blessings throughout the world, effecting a global change toward peace and harmony. Love would reign on our planet.

So let us radiate blessings from our heart. Swami Kriyananda offers a beautiful method: "Be joyful in meditation. Be peaceful. Bless all the world with your love. And, even walking down a city street, secretly send divine love and blessings to everyone you pass. You'll be surprised how many strangers will treat you as a friend."†

* *The Rubaiyat of Omar Khayyam, Explained*
† *Awaken to Superconsciousness*

The sunshine of grace

There is a second reason for "radiating blessings from your heart outward": success in meditation requires not only a good technique, such as *Hong-Sau*, but also the grace of the Heavens. And it is by giving that we receive that grace.

Imagine a person on that beautiful mountain trail, climbing upward toward the light. If, however, he thinks primarily about himself, there is a dense cloud above him, blocking the sunlight. His day will be foggy, his vision cloudy, his experience gray. If, on the other hand, he radiates blessings from his heart outward, suddenly that cloud is gone and the sun of grace shines brightly. With that warm sunlight he receives vitality, inspiration, and enlightenment for his journey.

It is helpful to often remember this essential teaching: "The channel is blessed by what flows through it." This spiritual law, like the laws of physics, remains immutable. Swami Kriyananda expresses it as follows: "Blessed are they who serve consciously as instruments of divine grace: for in their very giving they shall receive."*

A secret angel club

Have you heard? There is a rumor that of all those climbing the inner mountain of meditation, some have united to create a secret angel club of Grace Irradiators. Its members come from all over the world. They all meditate daily and then silently radiate light and blessings into this world from their hearts. Are you already a member? In that case you are one of the angels on earth.

If you are not yet a member, it is easy to join. Membership entails nothing more than meditating daily (which you might already do, given that you are reading this book); and secondly, silently radiating blessings to others during the day. If you start putting into practice these two requirements, you too will have become one of the precious angels on earth.

To help us increase our magnetism as Grace Irradiators, there are some special techniques to help us:

* *The Beatitudes*

1) Before meditation: a radiant Ananda Yoga asana

Before your *Hong-Sau* meditation, practice **ARDHA MATSYENDRASANA** (*Half Spinal Twist*). Fully enter into the experience by concentrating on the affirmation: **"I radiate love and goodwill to soul-friends everywhere."** By radiating blessings from your heart, you will have divine grace right there with you, uplifting your meditation.

2) During meditation: a heart-visualization

In the second part of the *Hong-Sau* technique, when you leave aside the mantra, absorb for some time its peaceful effect. Then focus on your heart and practice the following visualization by Swami Kriyananda.

> "Imagine in your heart [...] a kindly light. Send that light outward in rays of blessing to all. Mentally bless everyone near you; then, from your heart, send blessings to people in all lands, everywhere. Send rays of love to all creatures, to all things. Bless the rocks, the deserts, the vast oceans and high mountains. Surround the entire world in an aura of light, love, and joy. For everything is alive. All beings, all things manifest consciousness in varying degrees. They are part of the same eternal life that animates you. You will feel blessed, yourself, and filled with inner peace, the more you offer yourself in service as a channel of peace and blessings to all."*

As it is difficult to visualize while reading, you may want to listen to the following recording (www.crystalclarity.com/TMOY_links: "Radiate Light").

3) At the end of meditation: healing prayers

At the end of meditation, we always have the wonderful opportunity to "radiate blessings from our heart outward to all the world," by practicing healing prayers. Yogananda taught that we should rub the hands together strongly, energizing them, then lift them above the head and, while chanting OM three times, send healing energy from our hands to a person we visualize in front of us. And

---

* *Meditation for Starters*

we visualize that person healthy. We should always remember: the stronger the will, the stronger the flow of energy. We pray first for someone we love, then for someone we have trouble with and, finally, for the healing of our world.

4) Before leaving meditation: an affirmation

Before you leave your meditation, or at any other moment of the day, practice this affirmation by Yogananda, first loudly, then softer, then in a whisper, then mentally.

"As I radiate sympathy and good-will to others, I open the channel for God's love to come to me. Divine love is the magnet that attracts all blessedness."*

5) In free moments: a song of peace

Music helps our mind to absorb divine truths. Whenever you have a free moment you may listen to Swami Kriyananda's song, "Make Us Channels of Thy Peace." Its lyrics are part of the "Peace Prayer," attributed to St. Francis. The complete text includes these marvelous words: "For it is in giving that we receive, it is in pardoning that we are pardoned, and it is in dying that we are born to eternal life."†

* *Praecepta Lessons*
† *Awaken To Superconsciousness*

Here are the lyrics:

> **MAKE US CHANNELS OF THY PEACE**
>
> Lord most high our heav'nly father,
> All our lives we dedicate to Thee:
> All our labors, all our joys and woes,
> All our pleasure, all our melody.
> Make us each a channel of Thy peace:
> When in darkness, guide us from above;
> Where there's sorrow may we sow Thy joy;
> Where there's hatred may we share Thy love.

(www.crystalclarity.com/TMOY_links: "Make Us Channels of Thy Peace")

May this week bring about this important realization to you: that radiating blessings from your heart greatly improves your meditation and your daily practice of *Hong-Sau*.

WEEK 6 OF ADVANCED TRAINING: RADIATING BLESSINGS

Follow this sequence each day:

1) Practice the 20 *body-part recharging*.

2) Optionally practice the yoga asanas. Focus on *Ardha Matsyendrasana* (Half Spinal Twist).

3) Then follow the standard sequence of the *Hong-Sau* technique (Week 4 of Meditation Training), but practice *Hong-Sau* in the spiritual eye or in the spine. Try to go as deeply inside as you can.

4) Practice the second phase: look up with deep concentration to the spiritual eye, and meditate on whatever subtle perception comes to you. Enjoy it.

5) Your special training this week is radiating blessings: before you meditate, practice the guided heart-meditation by Kriyananda. Finish your meditation with a healing prayer. Practice the affirmation above if it inspires you.

6) Your second training concerns daily life: throughout the day silently radiate blessings into your environment.

WEEK 7 OF ADVANCED TRAINING

Overcoming Dry-Spells

"So long as man possesses a mind with its restless thoughts, so long will there be a universal need for yoga or control."

Autobiography of a Yogi

Are you in midst of a dry-spell?

This chapter is meant for the reader who has diligently gone through all the training of the preceding weeks, but without satisfying results. It is also intended for those difficult times when our meditations seem stuck: a situation every meditator experiences.

The question is: what can we do if our meditations have been very poor for quite some time? What if we are encountering a dry-spell and our meditations are quite simply not working? If that is your case, then this coming week is just for you. It offers a workshop designed to make your dry meditative land fertile again by irrigating it with fresh, revitalizing water.

The garden of inner meditation

A fruit tree produces a lot of fruit one year, but only a little the next. Meditation is similar: sometimes it is enjoyable and produces delicious fruit; sometimes there is no fruit, no enjoyment, no inner contact.

Yet–fortunately so –even when our meditations are only moderately fruitful, they still produce an abundance of benefits, both to us and to the world.

When inner enjoyment is lacking, we may decide to meditate less. Swami Kriyananda actually recommends that we: "Never meditate to the point of mental fatigue, strain, or boredom."

But "less" doesn't mean not at all. His advice is to remain regular, even if it means (as an exception) meditating only for 5 minutes.

> ### The SECRET of MEDITATION is...
>
> steadfastness: For the more you meditate, the more you will want to meditate, but the less you meditate, the less will you find meditation attractive.

The Meditation of Yogananda / 128

Become an inner gardener!

Sit up straight for a moment. Visualize within yourself an actual Inner Meditation Garden. This garden has the potential to produce many colorful flowers of amazing beauty, but if the flowers are to bloom, it requires your constant care and attention.

So, during the next seven days of our workshop, you will be asked to become an inner gardener, whose job it is to understand why his flowers are not flourishing as they should. Is it a lack of water? Is the earth too poor? Is there insufficient sunlight? Is some other plant inhibiting growth? Is the wind too strong for your delicate flowers? Are you correctly following the anciently prescribed rules of plant cultivation?

The gardener's three "Never-Rules"

First of all, there are the three *Never*-rules, which should be followed whenever our *Inner Meditation Garden* remains flowerless:

1) **Never quit.** Do less meditation for now, but remain regular. If you have already quit, begin again today.

2) **Never give up hope.** Don't resign yourself to the present situation. Your meditations *can* and *will* improve.

3) **Never feel bad about it.** These things happen and there is a solution for everything.

A Master-gardener will accompany you

A further rule for making our Inner Meditation Garden flower again is to invoke the help of a Master-gardener. For our workshop, let's choose Swami Sri Yukteswar, a saint of profound meditative wisdom. For example, as we have seen earlier, he teaches us that: "Outward longings drive us from the Eden within… The lost paradise is quickly regained through divine meditation."

If you haven't read Yogananda's *Autobiography of a Yogi* and do not know the great sage Sri Yukteswar, you may replace him with any sage teacher you know.

Should we look for results in meditation?

But is it actually wise to be result-oriented in our meditations? Is our goal to produce inner flowers a reasonable one? This is a good question and it requires a somewhat detailed answer.

As meditators, we need to find our personal point of equilibrium on a scale that balances two different approaches. The one approach is: "Accept whatever is. Don't worry about results." The other approach is: "Don't accept that something is forever. If there is a lack of results, do something about it."

Let us look at when the first approach is valid:

- Only a foolish gardener plants a seed and digs it up every day to check if his flower is growing ("Am I getting results?"). It's better to water the seed (to meditate) and then to relax and have trust.

- Nor does a wise meditative gardener expect any *specific* inner flower (experience) in his *Inner Meditation Garden*. Expectations are bound to disappoint. Instead we are taught to meditate in the spirit of karma yoga, without desiring any specific result: "Whatever comes of itself, let it come." Even if *nothing* comes, this is no problem. Meditation invariably brings good things, which are outside our conscious awareness. So just happily accept whatever comes.

- The telling sign of our meditative progress is not to be found in the inner flowers (experiences), but in our daily life. Are you becoming a more peaceful, inspired, loving, and luminous person? Then you are truly advancing, even though your meditations may reveal little to you. Once again: just happily accept those little meditative flowers.

Now let us look at when the other approach is valid:

- Settling for a few tiny flowers, while a paradisiacal inner garden ("the Eden within") is waiting for us, is not wise if it is because will-power and discipline are lacking. Yogananda encourages us to stimulate our will-power in this way: "Make today's meditation deeper than yesterday's and tomorrow's deeper than today's." To be sure, a continuous straight line of progress is unrealistic as nothing in this world develops linearly, day by day, without any bumps or setbacks. But what Yogananda is telling us is never to stagnate: we do want to see progress in our meditations. So do not accept where you are now as your permanent standard.

- We easily become set in our habits. Meditation is the highest form of *tapasya*, which literally means heat, resulting from the inner friction that is created when we work *against* our habits and egoic patterns. The ego resists meditation, which therefore necessitates a battle (*tapasya*). So again: do *not* accept a situation if some habit is impeding you. It's time to act.

Where is your personal point of equilibrium? Think about it. If you feel that you should add more weight to the approach on the other side of the scale, which says, "don't accept, but act," then the workshop below is for you—especially so if, as we said, you find yourself in the midst of a dry-spell. Our goal is to make our *Inner Meditation Garden* flower again.

Sri Yukteswar and his workbook

As good gardeners, our main question is: "What is it that is preventing my inner flowers from growing? What is making my soil so dry?"

To find out, let's now tune in to the wise advice of Sri Yukteswar. Imagine this majestic Master at your side, ready to help you in your efforts to find clarity. See him looking at you with his "beautiful deep eyes, smouldering with introspection, yet radiant with joy."* He asks you: "Do you really want to get to the bottom of it? Are you ready to face the truth about your meditations?"

Autobiography of a Yogi

If your answer is "yes," he hands you a *Meditation-Workbook For the Inner Gardener*. On its cover you see a beautiful lotus flower, symbolizing your soul.

The workbook contains seven self-analysis tasks, one for each of the next seven days. You will first find a **Meditation Sutra**, which creates the context for your daily introspection. It is often taken from Sri Yukteswar's book, *The Holy Science* (original edition of 1920, published in India by his disciple Atul Chandra Chowdhary). Following this, you will be guided into the **Meditation Garden Self-Analysis**. Once you have completed it, Sri Yukteswar will remind you that "what man has done, he can undo." To know how to "undo" your situation, you will practice a technique called **Intuitive Guidance**, which works like this: visualize Sri Yukteswar clearly in the spiritual eye, at the point between the eyebrows, and ask him the question you are given. After some time, enter into your heart chakra and intuitively feel his answer and guidance.

Sri Yukteswar asks you (let's imagine) not to rush through this process, but to go through the *Meditation-Workbook for the Inner Gardener* one day at a time.

Yoga asanas

If you practice the yoga postures, each day include **VASISTHASANA** (*Vasistha Pose*), which strengthens your mental focus. Affirm: **"The calm fire of my concentration burns all restlessness, all distraction."**

Now open the *Workbook* to find the first task for the first day:

> Providing good earth for the inner flowers:
> self-analysis concerning the **BODY**

---------------{ MONDAY }---------------

> **MEDITATION SUTRA:**
> "Asana means a steady (*sthira*) and pleasant (*sukham*) posture of the body"* OM.

Meditation Garden Self-Analysis:

Silence is the altar of Spirit. It begins with a steady body. Today as you meditate, observe yourself: for **how long do you sit motionless?** To answer this question, tick a box.

☐ 30 minutes   ☐ 15 minutes   ☐ 5 minutes   ☐ 2 minutes

To comprehend a thing, i.e. to clearly feel a thing in the heart, the practice of the aforesaid *asana*, the steady and pleasant posture, is absolutely necessary."† Relaxation, resulting in a "pleasant posture," is an important key for meditation. Today as you meditate, observe yourself. **How does your body feel as you meditate?** To answer this question, tick a box.

☐ Like a jellyfish   ☐ Pretty relaxed

☐ Somewhat relaxed   ☐ Tense

Intuitive Guidance:

If you ticked one of the last two boxes, apply the technique explained above and ask Sri Yukteswar: "What can I do to improve my physical stillness?" And: "What can I do to improve my relaxation?"

Write down the solution you receive.

* *The Holy Science* 3.15
† *The Holy Science* 3.18

{ TUESDAY }

> **MEDITATION SUTRA:**
> "A bent spine is the enemy
> of realization."* OM.

Meditation Garden Self-Analysis:

Today as you meditate, observe your asana (posture) attentively. **Is your spine straight all the time in meditation?**

To answer the question, tick a box.

☐ Yes, I am certain it is   ☐ I believe so   ☐ I am not sure   ☐ No

Intuitive Guidance:

If you ticked one of the last three boxes, apply the technique explained above and ask Sri Yukteswar: "How can I ascertain the situation and (if needed), improve the straightness of my spine?"

Write down the solution you receive.

> Giving water to the inner flowers:
> self-analysis concerning the **MIND**

{ WEDNESDAY }

> **MEDITATION SUTRA:**
> "The simple *thought* that
> we are not free is what keeps us
> from being free."† OM.

---

* *The Essence of Self-Realization*
† *Ibid*

The Meditation of Yogananda / 134

Meditation Garden Self-Analysis:

Our mind creates our reality, both inwardly and outwardly. It often becomes our saboteur if it holds harmful convictions, or negative mental "grooves." Today, as you meditate, observe yourself deeply. Honestly examine whether you have any of the following subconscious patterns in your meditative life:

- "I don't think I could ever reach a high state."
- "I don't deserve a saintly state."
- "Instinctively I am afraid of deeper states. I don't know where they would take me."
- "I fear that by really going deep I will change, and might become estranged from my family and friends."
- "I simply can't sit still."
- "Meditation is difficult and doesn't work for me."
- "I never have enough time to meditate."
- "Deep meditation is actually not all that important for me."
- "I am not a disciplined person because I don't have strong willpower."
- "I dislike discipline, regularity, being tied to a daily routine."

To answer the question, tick a box.
☐ I don't have any of these thought patterns   ☐ I might   ☐ I do

Intuitive Guidance:

If you ticked one of the last two boxes, apply the technique explained above and ask Sri Yukteswar: "What can I do to identify my particular pattern better? What can I do to change it? What thought or affirmation can I use to counteract it?"

Write down the solution you receive.

{ THURSDAY }

> **MEDITATION SUTRA:**
> "*Yama* is abstinence from cruelty, dishonesty, covetousness, unnatural living and unnecessary acceptance. *Niyama* is purity of body and mind, contentment in all circumstances and obedience to the precepts of the divine personages."*
> "The eight bondages are: hatred, shame, fear, grief, condemnation, race distinction, pedigree and the sense of respectability."† OM.

Meditation Garden Self-Analysis:

Our outer and inner life can't be separated. The quality of our daily life strongly influences the quality of our meditation. By removal of the above obstacles, "magnanimity of the heart results, making man fit for *asana* or correct posture, *pranayama* or prana control, and *pratyahara* or interiorization."‡

So today as you meditate, observe yourself and ask: "Do I manifest the above *yama* and *niyama*? And am I free of the above "eight bondages" in my life?"

To answer the question, tick a box.

☐ Yes, to a high degree ☐ Partly ☐ Not very much

Intuitive Guidance:

If you ticked one of the last two boxes, apply the technique explained above and ask Sri Yukteswar: "How can I develop the particular *yama/niyama* I need?" And: "How can I overcome this obstacle?"

* *The Holy Science*, 3.10-11
† *The Holy Science*, 3.13
‡ *The Holy Science*, 3.52

The Meditation of Yogananda / 136

> Providing sunlight for the inner flowers:
> self-analysis concerning the **SOUL**

---------------{ FRIDAY }---------------

> **MEDITATION SUTRA:**
> "In Him [Parambrahma, God, Spirit] is the origin of all knowledge, love, the root of all power and joy."* OM.

Meditation Garden Self-Analysis:

Devotion to God invites His indispensable help. "Hence the culture of this love, the heavenly gift, is the principle thing for the attainment of holy salvation and it is beyond doubt impossible for man to advance a step towards the same without this."† So today as you meditate, **ask yourself if your heart infuses your techniques** (devotion will be discussed soon, in a later chapter).

To answer the question, tick a box.

☐ It is effective for me   ☐ I feel some effect   ☐ It doesn't work for me

Intuitive Guidance:

If you ticked one of the last two boxes, apply the technique explained above and ask Sri Yukteswar: "How can I bring more devotion into my meditation? What will work for me?"

---

* *The Holy Science*, 1.2
† *The Holy Science*, 1.37

---{ SATURDAY }---

> **MEDITATION SUTRA:**
> "Pranayama means control over prana (life-force)."* OM.

Meditation Garden Self-Analysis:

Pranayama stills the mind and leads it toward interiorization (*pratyahara*). "If [man] can direct his organ of sense inward toward his Self at that time [of outer desire], he can satisfy his heart immediately."† Today at the beginning of meditation, practice pranayama (Measured Breathing is recommended) for a long time and **observe the effect of pleasant interiorization.**

To answer the question, tick a box.

☐ It is effective for me ☐ I feel some effect ☐ It doesn't work for me

Intuitive Guidance:

If you ticked one of the last two boxes, apply the technique explained above and ask Sri Yukteswar: "How can I practice in order to get deeper results?"

---{ SUNDAY }---

> **MEDITATION SUTRA:**
> "What is needed is a Guru, who will awaken in us devotion and perception of Truth."‡ OM.

Meditation Garden Self-Analysis:

In general, our meditation is deepened through attunement with a Guru. Today as you meditate, feel an advanced soul sitting at your side. Ask yourself: **"Does my meditation go better in this way?"** (This topic will be discussed in a later chapter).

To answer the question, tick a box.

☐ Definitively ☐ I feel some effect ☐ I don't feel a difference

Intuitive Guidance:

If you ticked one of the last two boxes, apply the technique explained above and ask Sri Yukteswar: "How can I explore this method of attunement better?"

* *The Holy Science*, 3.16   † *The Holy Science*, 3.45   ‡ *The Holy Science*, 1.17

The Meditation of Yogananda / 138

If you have followed this seven-day practice, you are done. Congratulations! Now ask yourself: "How does my *Inner Meditation Garden* appear? Am I observing the first colorful flowers? Am I emerging from the dry-spell?"

To inspire you to keep gardening, here is one of Yogananda's *Whispers From Eternity*:

TEACH ME TO STORE HONEY OF GOOD QUALITIES FROM ALL SOUL-FLOWERS IN THE HONEYCOMB OF MY HEART

In the summer days of life,
teach me to gather honey
from the flowers of all spiritual qualities
that blossom in the garden of truthful souls.

I will store the perfume of forgiveness
in the honeycomb of my heart:
the lotus fragrance of humility;
myrrh-scented devotion;
the rare honey of all soul-qualities.

And even though the snowflakes
of wintry experiences
and earthly separations whirl about me,
I shall seek Thee in the honeycomb of my heart
where often I have found Thee,
stealing the stored honey of my devotion.

Wherever Thou hast come—
in every place hallowed by Thy feet—
I will lie, touching Thy footprints.

Ah! there alone will I find a place
of true safety.

And for the future: should a dry-spell ever beset you again, return to your *Meditation Workbook For the Inner Gardener* and start over again.

WEEK 7 OF ADVANCED TRAINING: OVERCOMING DRY-SPELLS

Follow this sequence each day:

1) Practice the 20 *body-part recharging*.

2) Optionally practice the yoga asanas. Focus on *Vasishtasana* (*Vasishta* Pose).

3) Then follow the standard sequence of the *Hong-Sau* technique (Week 4 of Meditation Training), but practice *Hong-Sau* in the spiritual eye or in the spine. Your goal is calmness and inwardness.

4) During the second phase abandon the *Hong-Sau* technique, look to the spiritual eye and offer yourself into any perception you have.

5) Your special training this week is to **follow the workbook** outlined above, day by day.

Part 3 | *Hong-Sau* **for Self-realization**

> **Introduction to Part 3**
>
> **Self-Realization**
>
> "His [a swami's] goal is absolute unity with Spirit. Imbuing his waking and sleeping consciousness with the thought, 'I am He,' he roams contentedly, in the world but not of it."
>
> *Autobiography of a Yogi*

Self-realization

The *Hong-Sau* technique gradually makes our body, mind, and spirit happier, and adds depth to our life. This is wonderful in itself, but it is still not its highest purpose. Yogananda concentrated on the most elevated goal of meditation: the experience of bliss (*ananda*), which comes through Self-realization. This is where the inner path can finally lead us, if we so desire: transcending our limited personality and realizing our union with that Reality which has been called "God," "Spirit," or "Brahman."

Yogananda defined Self-realization in this way:

> "Self-realization is the knowing in all parts of body, mind, and soul that you are now in possession of the kingdom of God; that you do not have to pray that it come to you; that God's omnipresence is your omnipresence; and that all that you need to do is improve your knowing."*

---

* The Essence of Self-Realization

Please read this quote again, slowly and carefully, to digest it, as it presents the direction that we shall follow in the final part of this book. If that goal for now seems too distant and does not inspire you, please wait. Practice what you have learned so far; it has already been an amazing journey.

If, on the other hand, you sincerely feel ready, a new spiritual direction awaits you. Our goal will be pure Self-perception, which, at the same time, is God-perception. The wave gradually realizes that its reality, as a mere wave, is temporary. It slowly begins to experience that its reality lies not in its separateness as a wave, but in the ocean of which the wave is only a small manifestation.

Advanced yogis have taught throughout the centuries that knowing our true Self means at the same time knowing God. So: "The time of knowing God has come."

Satchidananda

Yogananda, representing these ancient yogic teachings and speaking from his own inner realization, defined God as *Satchidananda*, or ever existing, ever conscious, ever new bliss: "God may be defined in countless ways: as infinite Light, Power, Wisdom, and so forth. The most meaningful definition of all, however, in terms of life's most fundamental drives, is *Satchidananda*."*

Satchidananda is the omnipresent, blissful, and intelligent *Consciousness* out of which the entire creation evolved, like waves rising out of a silent ocean. "Everything exists only in consciousness.... The universe cannot be real except as a manifestation of that consciousness. If this is true, and it cannot but be true, then consciousness is the reality, and matter, the illusion."†

And what, then, is the soul? It is, as we said in a previous chapter, like a wave of the ocean: individualized *Satchidananda*. "We are made in the image of God," as the Bible tells us. Our soul is supremely happy. Happiness is our nature. Troubles arise because soul-joy has been forgotten and because we substitute it with the fleeting pleasures of the senses. All things, however, came from Bliss, or God. Eventually, all things must return to that bliss-state.

* *The Essence of Self-Realization*
† *Ibid*

Awaken *Kundalini*

Yogis whose ambition is to reach high spiritual goals speak about the necessity of awakening *kundalini*, a powerful energy at the base of the spine, and directing it upward. In Yogananda's tradition, the main technique for that awakening is Kriya Yoga. *Hong-Sau* prepares us by taking our awareness inside.

But even while practicing *Hong-Sau*, we can nudge the energy upward in our spine by our intention.

> The **SECRET** *of* **MEDITATION** *is...*
>
> to visualize the energy in the spine rising in joyful aspiration toward the point between the eyebrows.

Yogananda adds an essential point: "Every time you think good thoughts, the *kundalini* begins to move upward. Every time you hate people or hold harsh thoughts about them, the *kundalini* automatically moves downward. When you love others selflessly, or think kind thoughts about them, it moves up the spine. *Kundalini* is not awakened by techniques alone."* This is why the purification of our heart and mind, which we discussed in an earlier chapter, is so essential.

With the rising of the inner energy, our consciousness gets lifted toward union, or re-union, with Spirit.

The return home

The spiritual path of Self-realization, in fact, is nothing but a return to our natural inner state. We are all like the biblical prodigal son who left his home and his father (the inner paradise of union), wandered in foreign lands (in the senses, in separation), suffered poverty and hunger (spiritual lack and emptiness), and then returned home (experiencing the bliss of inner union again). The celebration of our homecoming, as the allegory in the Bible tells us, is great. The Father exclaims: "For this my son was dead, and is alive again; he was lost, and is found. And they began to be merry." (Luke 15:24)

---

* *The Essence of Self-Realization*

Our happy homeward journey, returning to Spirit, occurs through daily meditation. It is not a short journey, admittedly. But every step helps us to keep going "home."

We may start our *Hong-Sau* meditations, if we wish, with this invocation:

> Father, I have been Thy prodigal son.
> I have wandered away from Thy home of all power,
> but now I am back in Thy home of Self-realization.
> I want all good things that Thou hast,
> for they all belong to me. I am Thy child.*

A new religion?

Is meditation and Self-realization, then, a sort of new religion? By now it should be clear that it isn't. It is pure spirituality, the very opposite of any formal religion, which is based on beliefs, dogmas, and rituals. "Your beliefs won't save you," Yogananda explained simply. "Make spiritual practice, not belief, your 'dogma.'"†

The great Adi Shankaracharya, a famous teacher of Self-realization in ancient India, taught: "Religious works cannot destroy ignorance, for it is not in conflict with ignorance. Knowledge alone destroys ignorance, as light destroys dense darkness."‡

Spirituality is a path of inner realization. Our religious beliefs are secondary. Yogananda put it plainly: "Your religion is not the garb you wear outwardly, but the garment of light you weave around your heart. By outward garb I don't mean your physical raiment only, but rather the *thoughts and beliefs* in which you enclose yourself. They are not you. Discover who you are, behind those outer trappings, and you will discover who Jesus was, and Buddha, and Krishna. For the masters come to earth for the purpose of holding up to every man a reflection of his deeper, eternal Self."§

* *Metaphysical Meditations*
† *The Essence of Self-Realization*
‡ In *Atma-bodha*
§ *The Essence of Self-Realization*

"Self-realization," the Master predicted, "will someday be recognized as the essential truth of every religion in the world."* He even stated that "Self-realization is the only religion, the *true purpose* of all religions, and the *eternal message* of religion."†

The "*only* religion," as we said, happens within us: it means daily practice, mystical experience which is completely individual and personal. Long ago, original Christianity too was an inward practice, while the subsequent "churchianity" (a term coined by Yogananda) gave power and importance to institutionalism.

Yogananda himself created an organization, the *Self-realization Fellowship*, to serve as a hive where bees (seekers) can come to gather spiritual honey. He certainly never intended to create another form of "churchianity." In a recorded talk during one of his most important public events, the *Lake Shrine* dedication in 1950, when the governor of California and the media were present, one can hear him say: "I am not starting churches or other new cults. I don't believe in it... The greatest thing in the church movement is the building of colonies... Colonies where people can have their job, home, character-building, church, freedom, all at the same place."‡

Such "colonies" (communities) have been founded by his direct disciple, Swami Kriyananda, in America, Italy, and India. *Ananda* was the name given to these colonies. Their lifestyle is based on the universal teachings of Self-realization, emphasizing meditation and service, trying to maintain the sincere but completely undogmatic attitude of Yogananda: "Do not drift! Once you have found the universal truth, stick to it if you desire to grow. Universal and non-denominational is the truth of Self-realization."§

Devotion

Often, when followers of the "non-dual" philosophy (*Advaita Vedanta*) teach Self-realization, one finds no trace of devotion (*bhakti*). Yogananda's teaching, as we shall see, is the very opposite: it helps us to develop a strong

---

* *Conversations with Yogananda*
† *The Essence of Self-Realization*
‡ In his stated "Aims and Ideals," Yogananda included the creation of colonies (referred to in texts which appeared during his lifetime) in order "To spread a spirit of brotherhood among all peoples; and to aid in establishing, in many countries, self-sustaining world-brotherhood colonies for plain living and high thinking."
§ *East-West*, March 1934

love for God. But how can that be if He is at the same time our own true Self? Isn't that strange? Do we worship ourselves?

One time a philosophical visitor asked Yogananda exactly that question: "I am intrigued by the concept of Self-realization. However, I don't see how you tie it in with worship. Surely it isn't your teaching that we should worship ourselves!"

The Master replied: "One may affirm, 'I am infinite,' but without humility and devotion one slips all too easily into the error of thinking, 'I, in my exceptional greatness, am one with Infinity!' For this reason it is better, until one is highly advanced spiritually, not to think of God as, 'I,' but to address Him as 'Thou.' It is also more natural to think in this way. After all, as human beings we see others as separate from ourselves, even though, spiritually speaking, all are manifestations of the one divine Self. We don't ask a friend how he is by saying, 'How am I today?' To do so would be confusing even for a philosopher! Instead, we say, 'How are you?' An 'I-and-Thou' relationship with God is simpler, and less confusing. It is also much more satisfying to the human mind. And it is a relationship that God recognizes. The Lord responds to sincere devotion from His human children, never to proud self-affirmation."*

The following prayer creates a perfect devotional atmosphere for our journey toward Self-realization:

> "In the stillness of my soul
> I humbly bow before Thine omnipresence,
> knowing that Thou art ever leading me
> onward and upward on the path
> of Self realization."†

India's ancient treasure

Self-realization is, of course, not Yogananda's "trademark" or "invention." It is a central and ancient teaching of India, taught by countless great Masters throughout the centuries. In Sanskrit it is called *atma-gyana, atma-darshana, purusha-khyati* and various other names.

"Who am I?" is a question that India's saints have asked themselves for millennia. "What is my innermost essence?" Going deep within, they discov-

---
* *The Essence of Self-Realization*
† *Metaphysical Meditations*

ered that our true "I" (the soul, *atma*) is made of the same substance as God (Spirit, *Brahman*). Their glorious and liberating discovery can be duplicated by all of us, if we successfully enter into the inner silence, by going deep within during our *Hong-Sau* technique.

It is similar to peeling an onion: stripping away one layer after the other, one arrives at its innermost center. There its origin lies. Our deepest center—our own origin—is unexpectedly beautiful, more so than we have ever imagined. It is holy, eternal, free, full of bliss.

Adi Shankaracharya centuries ago sang six verses about the soul (*atma-shatakam*). Yogananda included one of them in his *Autobiography of a Yogi*:

> "Mind, nor intellect, nor ego, feeling;
> Sky nor earth nor metals am I.
> I am He, I am He, Blessed Spirit, I am He!
> No birth, no death, no caste have I;
> Father, mother, have I none.
> I am He, I am He, Blessed Spirit, I am He!
> Beyond the flights of fancy, formless am I,
> Permeating the limbs of all life;
> Bondage I do not fear; I am free, ever free,
> I am He, I am He, Blessed Spirit, I am He!"

The shift of our identity

In the West, the word "Self-realization" is often understood as the "fulfillment by oneself of the possibilities of one's character or personality." This is certainly a useful and honorable goal, but what is intended by the great yogis, as we have seen, is very different: it means realizing our potential as a soul, which is a part of God, just like the wave is a part of the ocean. It means experiencing the fact that our true life is eternal, without birth or death, ever perfect, ever loving, forever filled with joy. Think about it: we can never be destroyed, can never be hurt, nor could we ever end up in eternal hellfire. We are a part of God.

On the meditative path of Self-realization, this is our job: to transfer our identity from the little ego (our personality) to our infinite Self: God. Yogananda once explained it like this: "Self-realization means the realization that your true Self is not the ego, but God, the vast ocean of Spirit which manifested for a time the little wave of awareness that you now see as yourself."*

One time a student asked him: "What is the special purpose of your mission on earth?" The Master replied: "To awaken people to their need for Self-realization, through meditation, and through keeping good company, or fellowship, with other truth-seeking souls."†

Swami Kriyananda explained that "*Hong-Sau* will help you to convert ego-consciousness into the complete awareness of who and what you truly are: a manifestation of Pure Consciousness."‡

Meditation on our essence

During the *Hong-Sau* practice, therefore, meditate on this thought: "I *am* a soul and *have* a body."

All our troubles come from the fact that our soul has identified with our body, and therefore we suffer, physically die, and feel ourselves to be full of defects. But as we go deep in meditation we gradually realize that we are none of these things: not a man, not a woman, not our qualities or our defects.

Original Christianity and original Yoga

Jesus, too, taught that God must be realized within: "And when he was demanded of the Pharisees, when the kingdom of God should come, he answered them and said, The kingdom of God cometh not with observation. Neither shall they say, Lo here! or, lo there! for, behold, the kingdom of God is within you." (Luke 17, 20:21).§

Could it be true that Jesus was a yogi? He spent many of the unknown 18 years of his life in India and taught, according to Yogananda, a similar technique to Kriya Yoga.

---

* *The Essence of Self-Realization*
† *Ibid*
‡ *Awaken to Superconsciousness*
§ In modern Bible translations the Greek word "entos" is often translated as "among you." Some scholars, however, agree with earlier translations which used "within."

Jesus in fact transmitted to his followers this message of Self-realization: "Is it not written in your Law: 'I have said you are gods'?" (John 10:34) He may possibly have been referring to the Psalms, which declare: "You are gods; you are all sons of the Most High." (82:6)

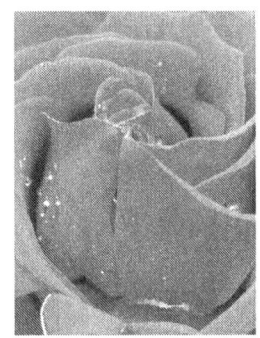

Later, St. Paul transmitted the same message of original Christianity: "Don't you know that you yourselves are God's temple and that God's Spirit dwells in your midst?" (1 Corinthians 3:16)

Jesus emphasized that he and his apostles, like all great Masters, spoke not from any Church doctrine, but from personal inner experience: "We speak that we do know, and testify that we have seen; and ye receive not our witness."*

His followers were asked to believe, but in order to achieve what Jesus himself had achieved: "Verily, verily, I say unto you, He that believeth on me, the works that I do shall he do also; and greater works than these shall he do; because I go unto my Father."†

Early Christians therefore meditated in caves and in the desert. They were mystics who knew how to enter into the inner silence, where they could personally experience God. "Be still and know that I am God." (Psalms 46:10)

> "Be still and know that I am God."
> ~Psalms 46.10 ~

Yogananda often quoted both the Bible and the Bhagavad Gita, emphasizing that the great Scriptures, if one examines them deeply, all teach the same truths. He added that his own teachings convey the "original Christianity of Christ and the original yoga of Krishna." That teaching is the path of Self-realization.

The *Hong-Sau* technique is designed for that purpose, as he explains in his *Yogoda* Lessons: "By continued proper practice you will feel a great calmness in you, and by and by you will realize yourself as a soul, superior to, and existing independently of, this material body."

---

* John 3:11
† John 14:12

WEEK 1 OF SELF-REALIZATION TRAINING

Hong-Sau *Peaks*

"Where there is duality by virtue of ignorance, one sees all things as distinct from the Self. When everything is seen as the Self, then there is not even an atom other than the Self."

Autobiography of a Yogi

Toward the Self

The training during this last part of the book is Self-realization: how to perceive ourselves as an immortal soul, not as a body.

Yogananda once stated: "By practicing the techniques I realize that my spirit is superconscious and I am not a mortal being. That is why Patanjali says it is necessary to get rid of inspiration and expiration, and you have been given the greatest techniques ever in the *Hong-Sau* and OM-techniques."*

From now on, therefore, when we practice *Hong-Sau*, we will do so with two specific goals:

> 1) **"I am He"**: our first goal is to affirm and feel constantly the meaning of *Hong-Sau* as we practice it: "I am He, I am Spirit." We train ourselves to feel more and more as a formless, ageless, genderless being. Does that mean we reject the body? Not at all. We consider it as an instrument, our house, our temple which we take good care of.
>
> 2) **Breathlessness**: our second goal is to gradually get closer to the breathless state, following Yogananda's guidance when he explains *Hong-Sau*: "By watching the breath, you metaphysically destroy the identification of the soul with the breath and the body. By watching the breath, you separate your ego from it and know that your body exists only partially by breath."†

Yogananda elsewhere points out: "To watch the breath is the preliminary step in controlling it, because then the consciousness of man *separates itself* from the involuntary bodily function of breathing, and gradually realizes itself as *distinct* from it." Often the Master emphasized:

> "Breathlessness is deathlessness."

To achieve these two goals, we will practice the *Hong-Sau* technique in two special ways. We will also practice all the other techniques we have learned towards that same end: Self-realization. Our constant training

---
* Patanjali Lessons. The OM-Technique is taught to disciples of Yogananda, while *Hong-Sau* is for the public: "Teach it to everyone who enters the door," the Master once said.
† Praecepta Lessons

will be to slowly shift our sense of identity from our personality, "I, Mary," to "I, pure consciousness." It is a long-term process which takes patience. Day by day, we will take small steps toward that goal.

Gradually our awareness will naturally expand as it becomes less bound to the body. It will take us toward a free state of consciousness, described in this affirmation by Swami Kriyananda: "I feel myself in the flowing brooks, in the flight of birds, in the raging wind upon the mountains, in the gentle dance of flowers in a breeze. Renouncing my little, egoic self, I expand with my great, soul-Self everywhere!"

So here is the way we will practice from now on:

1) Energization exercises for Self-realization

During the *Energization exercises*, try not only to feel, but to *identify* with the cosmic energy that enters into your body. In this way you train yourself to shift your identity from something mortal to something immortal. Yogananda explains: "More than all, Yogoda (*energization exercises*) will teach you that you are not the body, which is only your servant, but that you are the immortal life-energy."*

Affirm Yogananda's words: "Right beneath the flesh is a tremendous current. I forgot it, but now, by the pickax of Self-realization, I have dug that life-force up again. I and my Father are one. I am not the flesh. I am a bundle of electricity behind this body."†

2) Asana for Self-realization

If the yoga asanas are part of your daily *sadhana*, focus especially on *Sirshasana* (Headstand), which you must have learned properly from a teacher. Use it to shift your sense of identity from the body to the eternal soul. Affirm mentally in that posture: "I am He! I am He! Blissful Spirit, I am He!"

3) Prayer for Self-realization

Then sit down for meditation and offer a special prayer, such as this one by Yogananda: "Oh Spirit, May I know that I am not the body, not the blood, not the energy, not the thoughts, not the

---

* Praecepta Lessons   † Praecepta Lessons

mind, not the ego, not even the astral self; but that I am the immortal soul which illumines them all, remaining unchangeable in spite of their changes."*

4) Chant for Self-realization

Now chant Yogananda's song, "I am the sky": www.crystalclarity.com/TMOY_links

5) *Hong-Sau* Technique for Self-realization

AFFRMING THE SELF:

During the *Hong-Sau* technique, try with each inhalation to touch your formless Self. Apply the following instructions of Swami Kriyananda:

"As you chant *Hong* mentally with the incoming breath, feel that you are affirming not so much the little ego–the John Smith or Mary Green who is unique among human beings–but rather the Universal Man of which *you* are one expression. As you chant *Sau* mentally with the outgoing breath, feel that you are offering this self into the infinite Self or Spirit. Imagine your awareness expanding toward Infinity. Then as you chant *Hong* again, visualize the little self becoming infused with the consciousness of *Sau*, the Spirit, which you have just affirmed."†

ONENESS:

Reflect on these important words by Swami Kriyananda which you read earlier: "To repeat *Hong-Sau* mentally, particularly in conjunction with the breath, is to affirm again and again the truth that the little human ego is one with Brahman, the infinite Spirit: "*Hong Sau!* I am He! I am He!"‡

THE BELL:

He also recommends this technique: as you inhale, feel that the word "*Hong*" is like the tolling of a bell touching your sense of I. With "*Sau*" feel that the sound rings outward into the surrounding atmosphere.

BREATHLESSNESS:

Yogananda gave the following little-known instruction to Swami Kriyananda, which we too can follow with great benefit: "When

---

* *Metaphysical Meditations*   † *The Art and Science of Raja Yoga*   ‡ *Ibid*

watching the breath, I've previously taught *not* to control its flow. I wanted to tell you today, however, that that flow may be controlled to this extent: Between each breath, try, for that brief moment, to deepen the sense of release you feel from the need to breathe. Gradually, by natural degrees, those pauses will increase in length."*

Yogananda also taught: "Remember that the purpose of this practice is to increase naturally the intervals when the breath does not flow."†

6) After *Hong-Sau*

In that silence try to reach *dhyana*, union with an aspect of God. Feel yourself one with it.

The SECRET of MEDITATION is…

to visualize God in one of His
eternal aspects —as infinite light,
cosmic sound, eternal peace, love, or joy;
seek to unite yourself with Him
in that aspect.

---

7) Kriya Yoga for Self-realization

If you happen to be a Kriyaban (one who practices Kriya Yoga), practice it in a way that every breath carries you deeper inside, toward your formless Self. Again you may use Swami Kriyananda's words as guidance:

"The essence of meditation, the essence of spiritual progress, is *receptivity*. You don't have to accomplish anything, you have to receive that what already *is*, and that what you *are*. When you bring the energy up and down, try to feel that you are going deeper and deeper into your Self."‡

---

* *Conversations with Yogananda* † *Yogoda Lessons* ‡ In a talk on Kriya Yoga

8) Visualization for Self-realization

After finishing your *Hong-Sau* technique, practice the following visualization, again taken from Swami Kriyananda's book, *Raja Yoga*, consciously shifting your sense of identity towards a formless state:

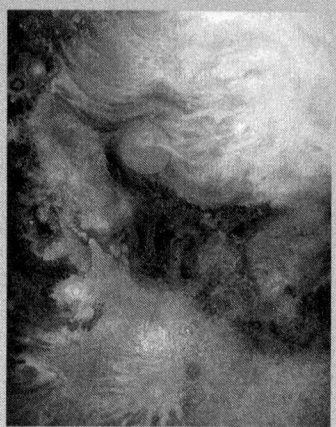

"In meditation it is good, in addition to devotional thoughts, to meditate on your own true, formless state. Think of a blue light (since blue is the color of the Christ consciousness). Visualize this light gradually expanding, filling your body, then the room in which you are sitting, your city, your country, your continent, the world. Visualize this light expanding beyond the world, filling the solar system, our galaxy, the entire manifested universe. See all things glimmering in this infinite light. The Scriptures say: '*Tat tuam asi*! Thou art that!' Dwell on the thought of your own infinite freedom. Why always affirm your temporary littleness? Patanjali said that divine realization is attained by awakening *smriti*, divine memory. In meditation the devotee at last remembers who and what He really is. *That* is the state of enlightenment. Any thought that feeds that divine memory will help to bring you back more and more to a recognition of the highest of all truths: '*Aham Brahm asmi*—I am Brahman!'."

9) Memorize the poem, "Samadhi"

Read and try to memorize Yogananda's poem, *Samadhi*. During the final part of your meditation, repeat at least some phrases mentally. Yogananda in fact recommended: "Repeat it daily. Visualize yourselves in that infinite state; identify yourselves with it. For *that alone* is what you really are!"* Here it is:

---

* The New Path

SAMADHI

Vanished the veils of light and shade,
Lifted every vapor of sorrow,
Sailed away all dawns of fleeting joy,
Gone the dim sensory mirage.
Love, hate, health, disease, life, death,
Perished these false shadows on the screen of duality.
Waves of laughter, scyllas of sarcasm, melancholic whirlpools,
Melting in the vast sea of bliss.
The storm of *maya* stilled
By magic wand of intuition deep.
The universe, forgotten dream, subconsciously lurks,
Ready to invade my newly-wakened memory divine.
I live without the cosmic shadow,
But it is not, bereft of me;
As the sea exists without the waves,
But they breathe not without the sea.
Dreams, wakings, states of deep *turia* sleep,
Present, past, future, no more for me,
But ever-present, all-flowing I, I, everywhere.
Planets, stars, stardust, earth,
Volcanic bursts of doomsday cataclysms,
Creation's molding furnace,
Glaciers of silent x-rays, burning electron floods,
Thoughts of all men, past, present, to come,
Every blade of grass, myself, mankind,
Each particle of universal dust,
Anger, greed, good, bad, salvation, lust,
I swallowed, transmuted all
Into a vast ocean of blood of my own one Being!
Smoldering joy, oft-puffed by meditation
Blinding my tearful eyes,
Burst into immortal flames of bliss,
Consumed my tears, my frame, my all.
Thou art I, I am Thou,
Knowing, Knower, Known, as One!

Tranquilled, unbroken thrill, eternally living, ever-new peace!
Enjoyable beyond imagination of expectancy, *samadhi* bliss!
Not an unconscious state
Or mental chloroform without wilful return,
Samadhi but extends my conscious realm
Beyond limits of the mortal frame
To farthest boundary of eternity
Where I, the Cosmic Sea,
Watch the little ego floating in Me.
The sparrow, each grain of sand, fall not without My sight.
All space floats like an iceberg in My mental sea.
Colossal Container, I, of all things made.
By deeper, longer, thirsty, guru-given meditation
Comes this celestial *samadhi*.
Mobile murmurs of atoms are heard,
The dark earth, mountains, vales, lo! molten liquid!
Flowing seas change into vapors of nebulae!
AUM blows upon vapors, opening wondrously their veils,
Oceans stand revealed, shining electrons,
Till, at last sound of the cosmic drum,
Vanish the grosser lights into eternal rays
Of all-pervading bliss.
From joy I came, for joy I live, in sacred joy I melt.
Ocean of mind, I drink all creation's waves.
Four veils of solid, liquid, vapor, light,
Lift aright.
Myself, in everything, enters the Great Myself.
Gone forever, fitful, flickering shadows of mortal memory.
Spotless is my mental sky, below, ahead, and high above.
Eternity and I, one united ray.
A tiny bubble of laughter, I
Am become the Sea of Mirth Itself.

Since you probably haven't memorized it yet, you may use the recording from Swami Kriyananda's CD, *Metaphysical Meditations*: www.crystalclarity.com/TMOY_links

WEEK 7 OF SELF-REALIZATION TRAINING: DEEPEN THE PRACTICES

Follow this sequence each day:

1) Practice the 20 *body-part recharging*, following the instructions given in this chapter.

2) Optionally perform the yoga asanas, with the attitude described. Focus on *Sirshasana* (Headstand).

3) Use the prayer and chant which have been described.

4) Then follow the standard sequence of the *Hong-Sau* technique (Week 4 of Meditation Training), practicing *Hong-Sau* in the spine or in the spiritual eye. Every day apply one of the special *Hong-Sau* suggestions described in this chapter.

5) Practice the second phase as always: looking up with concentration, absorb yourself in any quality you may feel. You are that.

6) Your special training this week is to apply the techniques in a new way, **dedicating yourself fully to Self-realization**.

7) Your second training concerns daily life: take some time to learn at least a part if not the whole of the poem ***Samadhi***. Recite it mentally when you have a free moment.

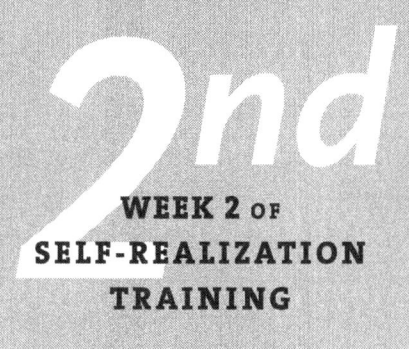

WEEK 2 OF SELF-REALIZATION TRAINING

Devotion

"*Casting aside every* inferior attachment, Ananda Moyi Ma offers her sole allegiance to the Lord. Not by the hairsplitting distinctions of scholars but by the sure logic of faith, the childlike saint has solved the only problem in human life — establishment of unity with God."

Autobiography of a Yogi

Devotion

Devotion has already been mentioned numerous times in this book. This week, however, we will give it our full attention, focusing on this alone. The training is to infuse our meditations with the power of the heart.

What is devotion? For a moment delve into your heart. Usually it is *outwardly* directed, to a child, to a person, to nature, to a hobby. But when our heart's energy flows upward to a higher reality, it becomes devotion. It is one of Patanjali's ten *yamas* and *niyamas*, called *Ishwara pranidhana*, meaning "dedication to *Ishwara* (God)."

Love is the fuel

Love, as we all know, is a powerful motor in life. What can stop us when with all our heart we deeply love something? *Nothing*. And what can stimulate our will and enthusiasm more than the passion of love? Yet again, *nothing*. What has a stronger impact on our determination than intense love? *Nothing*. A woman can even miraculously lift a car with her hands to save her father.

In meditation, too, love is a magic fuel which greatly empowers our efforts. Equipped with it, *nothing* will be able to stop our progress.

Think about it: why is it hard to concentrate deeply during our meditation? The probable answer is because it lacks the magic fuel of love. Without the heart, the mind too is weak and becomes distracted. On the contrary, if we love something, it is hard not to concentrate on it. In the cinema, for example, if

we love the film, we suddenly become perfect yogis: fully and naturally concentrated.

Love, in other words, is the key to our concentration during the *Hong-Sau* technique.

Maybe this is why Swami Kriyananda had his own way of practicing *Hong-Sau*: he inwardly used an unorthodox translation of the mantra: not "I am He," but "I am Thine."* In this way, the technique becomes an act of the heart, of devotion. You may try it to see if it helps you too.

---

* *Lessons in Self-Realization*

God's vow of silence

Yogananda taught us to pray like this: "Thou art our Father, we are Thy children. Teach us to love Thee as Jesus loved, as Mohammed loved, and as Christna [Krishna], and our great Gurus loved Thee. O God, teach us to love Thee with the intoxicating love of the saints, that we may realize that Thou are the ocean and our love is the wave. Teach us no more to pray with words, but with our souls. Father, break Thy vow of silence. Speak to us through our thoughts."*

Let us remember that everyone can freely think of "God" in whatever way inspires him. You can think of Him as the ocean of Love, if this moves your heart. Maybe it inspires you to think of an ever-loving Divine Mother. An atheist may think of the highest potential he can imagine for himself. A Christian can think of a Heavenly Father. There is no dogmatic restriction. The only indispensable ingredient is love.

Yogananda says: "He doesn't need from us carefully contrived theological definitions. And He doesn't want prayers that are chiseled to perfection lest they give offense to His imperial ears. He wants us to love Him in all simplicity, just like children."†

How to dry a wet matchstick?

Here is our goal: "You must sit and pray and cry and churn the ether with your yearning until all space is aflame with your devotion."‡

How can we develop such fiery devotion? How can we increase our passion when we sit down for our *Hong-Sau* meditation? How can we dry up the "wet matchstick" of our heart, which for so long has been unable to light the fire of divine aspiration?

One major tool is chanting. In time it naturally inflames our heart: maybe not immediately, but slowly, song after song, chant after chant, over the months and years.

"Chanting is half the battle," is one of Yogananda's well-known sayings.

Once we start offering melodies upwards from our heart, we have started lighting that warm fire of love and devotion, called bhakti.

---

* *Inner Culture*, September 1936
† *The Essence of Self-Realization*
‡ Patanjali Lessons

> ### The SECRET of MEDITATION is...
> ### singing to God, out loud or silently, to awaken devotion in the heart.

Swami Kriyananda explains the power of chanting in his own inimitable way: "Words are thoughts crystallized. Melodies are the resonance of the heart's aspirations. Harmonies deepen the emotional power of those aspirations. And rhythms ground those aspirations in the present. Combining thought, melody, and rhythm in a spiritual discipline can provide a powerful force for awakening."*

A chanting workshop: "Warming My Heart Aflame"

Do you have a guitar, a harmonium, or a keyboard at home? Or do you have a good recording of devotional chants? This week you will be required to make use of your voice, no matter how little you have used it before. Theory will never warm our heart. Only practice will. As the German poet Goethe said: "Grey, dear friend, is all theory, but the golden tree of Life springs ever green."

So you are therefore invited to a special chanting workshop. Here is what we do: we will use one of Yogananda's chants, which he called *Cosmic Chants*, to stimulate devotion. It doesn't matter if you are a good singer or not, or if you sing in tune or not. God watches the heart. Love is always beautiful.

> **1)** First carefully read the following words by Yogananda, taken from his book *Cosmic Chants*:
>
> "One who repeats these *Spiritualized Songs* or *Cosmic Chants* with ever-increasing devotion will find a more direct way to contact God than by the repetition of songs which are the outcome of blind sentiment and not of God-communion. These chants properly repeated will bring God-communion and ecstatic joy, and through these the healing of body, mind, and soul."

---

* *Awaken to Superconsciousness*

2) Then invoke the divine Presence with a special prayer:

"O Spirit, beloved Father, Oversoul of the Universe, Spirit of Spirits, Friend of Friends: teach me the mystery of my existence! Teach me to worship Thee in breathlessness and in deathlessness. In the fire of devotion burn away my ignorance. In the stillness of my soul—come, Spirit, come! Possess me and teach me to feel Thy immortal presence in and around me. Come, Spirit, come! Come, Spirit, come!"*

3) Afterwards, listen to switch on one of the *Cosmic Chants*, "Door of My heart," and pay attention to how Swami Kriyananda sings it (on the website www.crystalclarity.com/TMOY_links). Tune into the heart's energy, which he offers upward to the divine Presence.

If you don't play an instrument, listen to the same chant again and sing along with Swami Kriyananda. Try to kindle the fire of your heart with your chanting. Alternatively, take your harmonium or guitar and play the chant. Here are the chords:

DOOR OF MY HEART

```
C      dm G   F                am
Door of My heart, open wide I keep for you  |:2

F       dm   am     dm   F               am
Wilt Thou come, wilt Thou come, just for once come to me  |:2

C         dm G   F                am
Will my days fly away, without seeing Thee my Lord |:2

F       dm   am     dm  F                am
Night and day, night and day, I look for you night and day |:2
```

Repeat this chant several times. Open your heart consciously as you sing. You should gradually perceive a sense of warmth. Practice sweet devotion. Let your voice express your feeling.

---

* *Whispers From Eternity*

We all can learn to play an instrument. The harmonium is not difficult to play.

4) After the chant, meditate using the *Hong-Sau* technique. Infuse your meditation with the awakened love of your heart. Feel the new quality which now permeates your practice.

In addition, each day of this week, as you practice devotional chanting in your meditation, use one of the devotional Secrets of Meditation by Swami Kriyananda:

MONDAY
The **SECRET** *of* **MEDITATION** *is...*

offering yourself up wholly to the Lord,
holding nothing back.

TUESDAY
The **SECRET** *of* **MEDITATION** *is...*

loving God in whatever form you hold especially dear,
and praying, "God—my Father, Mother,
dearest Friend—I am Thine forever: Thine alone!"

WEDNESDAY
The **SECRET** *of* **MEDITATION** *is...*

dwelling on the thought of God's love for you,
and destroying in a bonfire of devotion
any lingering doubts.

THURSDAY
The **SECRET** *of* **MEDITATION** *is...*

to pray with deep faith—not as an outsider to heaven,
but as one whose true, eternal home is heaven.

FRIDAY
The SECRET *of* MEDITATION *is...*

visualizing yourself seated
at the heart of eternity;
sending rays of divine love outward
from your center to all the universe.

SATURDAY
The SECRET *of* MEDITATION *is...*

offering gifts of love upward from your heart to
the Christ Center between the eyebrows,
like the soaring flames in an all-purifying fire.

SUNDAY
The SECRET *of* MEDITATION *is...*

to visualize God in one of His eternal aspects—
as infinite light, cosmic sound, eternal peace,
love, or joy; seek to unite yourself
with Him in that aspect.

As you fill your heart with devotion this week, see how your *Hong-Sau* technique suddenly becomes more colorful, beautiful, deep, and inspiring.

Questions and Answers

Question: Which chants should I use?

Answer: Yogananda recommended using his *Cosmic Chants*, as they are permeated with high spiritual vibrations. He chanted each of them until he was in God-communion, spiritualizing them consciously. The subtle fact is that a chant, just like a house, absorbs vibrations. Each of the *Cosmic Chants* is a vibrational bridge on which we can walk toward the Infinite. Swami Kriyananda once stated: "My chants too are spiritualized, simply to a lesser degree."

What about Indian chants? Sanskrit chants and mantras are powerful, beautiful, and inspiring for many seekers. You may follow your own inspiration and chose whatever touches and uplifts your heart most. If, however, you feel Yogananda to be your spiritual guide, use his chants.

Musically-trained persons can create their own chants, provided they truly come from the heart and are not mentally constructed.

Question: Is it best to chant alone or in a group?

Answer: Chanting can be done both alone and in a group. Do you know a group nearby which meets to chant together? That would be a great help for the inner fire of your heart. Group chanting has a special power, provided that people sing not to have fun, but to sincerely express their love for the divine Presence. Yogananda writes:

"The *sankirtans* or musical gatherings are an effective form of yoga or spiritual discipline, necessitating deep concentration, intense absorption in the seed thought and sound. Because man himself is an expression of the Creative Word, sound has the most potent and immediate effect on him, offering a way to remembrance of his divine origin."*

In a group of people chanting sincerely, sometimes a tangible divine atmosphere permeates the air. The Infinite reacts to singing, it seems: "God loves the gentle songs coming from our hearts."†

If there is no group, chanting alone is just as beautiful and effective. It has a more intimate character.

* *Autobiography of a Yogi*   † Patanjali Lessons

The Meditation of Yogananda / 170

Question: Can I really feel devotion if I am just learning how to play and chant?

Answer: If you are not used to chanting, at first you might feel a little uneasy, almost as if you were stepping unsteadily on a new and unknown terrain. Something in you might say: "It's not me." And if you are learning an instrument, you obviously have to concentrate on the technique.

But once you get into it, your devotion will gradually grow and you will discover a precious secret of meditation.

Question: How many chants should I learn?

Answer: Fortunately, we don't need to learn many songs. In fact, "the more the better" is not a good idea. "The fewer the deeper," is better advice. It is, therefore, best to pick just one chant, or two, those which inspire you most. Sing them over and over, making them more and more your own. This repetition will spiritualize those songs for you. Swami Kriyananda did precisely that, always singing the same one or two chants, year after year. But it was real chanting: he sometimes began to cry from his deep devotion as he sang.

One can deeply feel his overflowing heart on one of his recordings, "My Lord I will be Thine Always" on the album *Kriyananda Chants Yogananda*. Listen carefully, until the end, and absorb his sincere devotion. (You can find it here: https://www.crystalclarity.com/TMOY_links/)

Question: Is there a specific method to chanting?

Answer: Yes. Singing from the heart is both an art and a science. Nobody can teach us the art: that is something we need to explore by ourselves. But the science, the technique, is something we can learn. In his book Cosmic Chants (1938), Yogananda explains it in this way:

> "The five states in chanting are **conscious chanting aloud—whisper chanting—mental chanting—subconscious chanting—superconscious chanting**. Subconscious chanting becomes automatic with internal consciousness only, when the mind automatically repeats a chant in the background of thought and activity…. Each devotee should set aside a regular time for singing these songs. Chant first **aloud**, then **whisperingly**, then **mentally**. A group, gathered together in the name of God can take one of these chants, singing it together **loudly**, with piano or organ accompaniment, then more **slowly** [**softly**], then singing in a **whisper** without any accompaniment, and finally **mentally** only, In this way deep God-perception can be reached singly or together."

Swami Kriyananda expands on these stages of chanting:*

LOUD CHANTING

"Loud chanting does have its place. It is good at the start of meditation…to command attention from our own minds. For loud chanting creates a magnetic flow. Like a mighty river, it can dissolve the eddies of thought and feeling that meander idly along the banks of the mind. Like a magnetic military leader, it commands attention from your thought-soldiers and fires them with zeal."

SOFTER CHANTING

"Once you've got their attention, chant more softly, more inwardly. Direct your energy upward, now, from the heart to the Spiritual Eye."

WHISPERED CHANTING

"Once your conscious mind is wholly engaged in chanting, bring it down into the subconscious by whispering. While chanting in the subconscious, offer the chant there, too, up to superconsciousness at the point between the eyebrows, until you feel your entire being vibrating with the words, the melody, and the rhythm."

MENTAL CHANTING

"At last, chant only mentally, at the point between the eyebrows. Let your absorption lift you into superconsciousness. Once it does so, and once you receive a divine response, you will have spiritualized the chant. From then on, any time you sing the chant it will quickly carry you again to superconsciousness as if on a magic carpet."

Then mediate with your heart aflame. Concentrate on the heart quality. Quality is more important than quantity. When the heart is no longer in your meditation, you may chant again, adding another drop of love: many drops make an ocean!

* *Awaken to Superconsciousness*

Question: What are the main guidelines for chanting?
Answer: Here they are. All quotes are from Swami Kriyananda.*

1) Chant with a clear purpose in mind

"The art of chanting correctly is, first, to practice it with full awareness of its inner purpose. That purpose is not to awaken sentiments or to stir up the emotions. It is to focus the heart's feelings and raise them toward superconsciousness."

2) Fill the chant with your heart

"To repeat a chant mechanically, in a singsong manner, has virtually no spiritual value." Our heart must sing, more than our voice.

3) Let your chant be a prayer

"Spiritual chanting is heartfelt prayer, deepened by the dimension of music and by the building power of repetition. Repetition is not for the purpose of getting the Lord's attention: It is to deepen the intensity of one's own prayer."

Question: Can I also chant during my daily life?
Answer: It would be marvelous: "To spiritualize a chant, keep it rotating in the mind—for days at a time if necessary, not only in meditation, but as you go about your daily activities. This practice is also called japa."† "Try incorporating chants and japa into your daily spiritual practices. You will soon discover why Yogananda said that 'Chanting is half the battle.'"‡

Yoga asanas

If you choose to practice the asanas, focus on the devotional **YOGA MUDRA** (*Symbol of Yoga*). Affirm: **"I am Thine. Receive me."**

---

* *Awaken to Superconsciousness*
† *Ibid*
‡ *The Art and Science of Raja Yoga*

WEEK 2 OF SELF-REALIZATION TRAINING: DEVOTION

Follow this sequence each day:

1) Practice the 20 *body-part recharging*.

2) Optionally practice the yoga asanas. Focus on *Yoga Mudra* (Symbol of Yoga).

3) Use the prayer and chant described in the Chanting workshop.

4) Then follow the standard sequence of the *Hong-Sau* technique (Week 4 of Meditation Training), practicing *Hong-Sau* in the spine or in the spiritual eye. Apply one of the suggestions described in Week 1 of Self-Realization Training.

5) Give much energy to the second phase: look upward in soul-yearning.

6) Your focus this week is: practice **filling your heart with devotion** as you chant, pray, meditate.

7) Your second training concerns daily life. **Practice devotion**: practice *japa*, or an inner song, or a prayer.

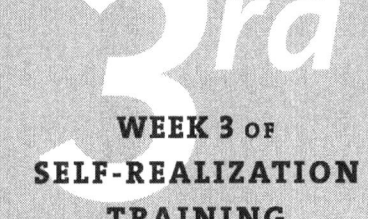

WEEK 3 OF SELF-REALIZATION TRAINING

Cooperating With Grace

"One night, in this very room, I had a vivid dream. Glorious angels floated in unimaginable grace above me. So realistic was the sight that I awoke at once; the room was strangely enveloped in dazzling light."

Autobiography of a Yogi

The Light of Grace

Our soul is, in reality, free, joyous, and powerful spirit. But in our present egoic state—i.e. in which our soul identifies with the body and in which we perceive ourselves as "John" or "Mary"—it is as though we had built an ego-house around our spirit, complete with walls and roof. In this way, it receives much less of the Sun's vitalizing light.

This house with its walls and roof separates us from our source of power, which means that, despite our efforts here on earth, we remain all too human and, as humans, are weak. Our personal efforts alone will never suffice to save us from the consequences of our failings, or to raise us into the realm of Spirit. In short, we need the help of the Sun's light.

This powerful light of the sun is God's grace. In fact, according to Yogananda, the spiritual path is 25% self-effort, 25% the blessings of one's Guru and 50% the grace of God.

Therefore, if our desire, by use of the *Hong-Sau* technique, is to reach greater heights, then Divine grace is an essential ingredient for our success. But how are we to attract it to us?

The indispensable requirement for receiving it is our love. But that love, as we shall see during this week, can be effectively deepened by yoga techniques, which help us to receive God's grace in greater abundance.

> *The* **SECRET** *of* **MEDITATION** *is...*
>
> receptivity to God's grace,
> in full awareness that God's power alone
> can liberate the soul.

The essence of yoga

Throughout his life, Swami Kriyananda taught that "yoga is cooperation with grace." This inner cooperation is actually the very essence of all yoga techniques and, indeed, of the entire yogic science.

He wrote an extensive series of "Lessons in Self-realization," (not yet published) at the end of which, as a conclusion, he stated: "Everything I have written about the spinal channels; the inner light; watching the breath to achieve concentration; gazing at the point between the eyebrows; raising the energy in the spine: well, *everything* in these lessons is only a means of cooperating with the way divine grace actually works in the body."

Grace, the Masters teach, is not some capricious divine favor. Yes, it is the gift of God's blessing, but it is one that we can consciously draw on by using specific yogic practices. Grace, far from being God's whim, relates to His law of love and receptivity. It flows (both momentarily and constantly) into all those who have inwardly learned how to receive it. Yoga techniques teach us how to open our inner curtains, so to speak, to the sunlight of grace, which perpetually shines upon us.

The inner skylight

But where are these curtains that we have to open? We won't find them on the ground floor of our inner house. Grace shines through the skylight in our inner "roof" and, consequently, we need to go upstairs. In other words, our job is to elevate our energy and consciousness if we want to receive the light of grace. During all the techniques suggested by Yogananda, the eyes are constantly raised in order to elevate our consciousness toward the skylight. All the techniques take us "to the roof," because only in an elevated state (of the soul) are we able to open our curtains and let the sunlight of God's grace enter.

However, have you ever asked yourself what grace actually is? Yogananda gives us an enlightening answer: "It is *God's power*," he says, "as distinct from any lesser power. Because God is the only Reality, His also is the only power in existence. Seen in this light, our merely human efforts are illusory. It is His power, even when we draw on it unconsciously, that accomplishes everything that we achieve in life. And our failures are due to lack of attunement on our part with that power. God's grace flows into us the more we open ourselves to Him. It doesn't come to us from outside. It is the operation, from within, of our own higher reality. Grace comes the more we live in soul-consciousness and the less we live centered in the ego."*

* *The Essence of Self-Realization*

The two directions of grace

Grace, or "God's power," flows in two directions. The first direction is *outward*, from God toward the world. Consider this: we are living solely by His grace at this very moment. We unconsciously exist, act, and breathe by virtue of His grace all the time, and His grace "accomplishes everything that we achieve in life." The more we elevate our consciousness, however, the more we can become *aware* of that grace, learning how to become channels of it.

The great masters and saints are our role models as they are powerful channels of God's grace flowing outward into the world. In the Bible, St. Stephen (the first Christian martyr) provides an example: "And Stephen, full of grace and power, was doing great wonders and signs among the people."* We are encouraged to do likewise: "Each of you should use whatever gift you have received to serve others, as faithful stewards of God's grace in its various forms."†

The second flow is *inward*, from the world back to God. It is a liberating power, which Swami Kriyananda describes as follows: "It is divine grace alone, finally, that lifts the devotee out of delusion and into Divine Perfection."‡ In the Bhagavad Gita (18:73) Arjuna exclaims: "My delusion has been demolished! I have, by Your grace, O Krishna, regained the memory of my soul [*smriti*]."

To understand these two directions, think of the sun: on the one hand, its nourishing sunrays stream *outward* toward all creatures, who receive the gift gratefully; on the other hand, its mighty gravitational pull attracts everything *inward*, back into itself.

Two strange yogis

There is a story of two great—but strange—yogis in India. One of them kept his arms constantly extended upward to the sky, chanting everywhere he went:

---

* Acts, 5:6
† 1 Peter 4:10
‡ *Rays of the Same Light*

"God's grace, oh God's grace." The other yogi chanted that very same song, but constantly kept both arms extended forward in blessing. One day the two yogis met and were appalled by each other. The one with the arms extended upward exclaimed: "What is this bizarre gesture of yours all about? God's grace takes us *inward*, lifting us up into His light." The other, who had his arms extended forward, replied: "What kind of weird yogi are you? God's grace blesses others *outwardly*, through us." A heated argument ensued. It was a rather curious scene, with agitated arms brandished ever more upward and ever more forward. Fortunately, at that moment, Lord Krishna appeared and smiled: "O great souls, be at peace. From today onwards, both of you shall hold one arm up, *inwardly* soaring toward Heaven with divine grace; and let your other arm be extended forward, *outwardly* sharing divine grace with the world." The two yogis followed his advice and soon entered into a state of boundless grace, living in it blissfully ever after. So, dear reader, if you should happen to meet an unusual yogi with one arm extended upward and the other forward, you'll know precisely what he is up to!

The upward flow of grace within us

Grace, as Yogananda explains above, "doesn't come to us from outside," but operates "from within." In our body, just as in the universe, we can discover two currents of grace. One is a current of *upward* rising energy, which carries us toward the inner sun (the sun in our body is the spiritual eye). We all instinctively know the feeling: when we are uplifted, as if on wings of inspiration, and automatically look upward. When this upward current becomes strong, it becomes a river of bliss. In meditation, if the meditator is deeply interiorized, this upward flow of grace in the spine carries him to the paradise of divine union. A light may appear, or divine love may be felt, or there may be a feeling of expansion, or a sound may be heard. This must have been the experience of John Newton, when he wrote the famous song, *Amazing Grace*, in which he sings, "how sweet the sound." It was the sound of grace, which he perceived during a state of divine inner upliftment.

As a young monk, Swami Kriyananda soon learned the lesson: "I had thought of myself as flying by my own strength, forgetting that, to soar high, the devotee must allow himself to be lifted on breezes of God's grace... Cooperation with the guru's efforts, and with divine grace, means doing what one can, personally, to direct energy *upwards through the spine*."*

The downward flow of grace within us

The second current of grace flows in the opposite direction, i.e. "downward from above," from the inner sun (spiritual eye) into the body. And again we all know the feeling. It is the feeling we have when we automatically turn our palms up, to receive a descending flow of blessings. It is the sensation experienced in all spiritual cultures throughout the world: the sensation of receiving a cascade of God's grace from above, which enters into us, filling us.

Yoga techniques, as we said, are designed to help us cooperate with grace, but how?

Swami Kriyananda gives an illuminating answer: "The essence of spiritual development is, by deep calmness, humility, and love to increase our *receptivity*. Yoga practice is in this respect no different from other spiritual practices. Its difference lies in its practicality and in the awareness it develops of *subtle energy currents* in the body. This awareness helps one to attune himself to the inner *flow of divine grace*, enabling him to *cooperate* with that flow which, otherwise, he might find himself resisting in sheer surprise, owing to his ignorance of it, or to any fear he may have of the unknown." †

Each one of the techniques of Yogananda's path of *Self-realization* cooperates with grace in a specific way:

* *The New Path*
† *The Promise of Immortality*

1) Energization Exercises: a first step toward grace

You have learned the 20 body-part recharging technique, which is part of the *energization exercises*. As you practice it this week, let your attitude be: "The flow of energy that I receive is grace descending into me."

Swami Kriyananda in fact teaches that tuning into this flow of energy is a first practical step toward perceiving grace: "Wisdom, love, joy, peace, all divine qualities, as well as energy, are implied in the flow of divine grace. But they are perceived first, and most easily, in their lower manifestation, as energy. By learning how to attune oneself to the cosmic energy, one learns the secret of divine attunement on all levels."*

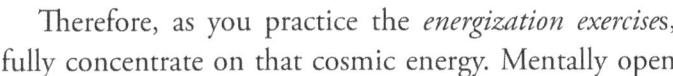

Therefore, as you practice the *energization exercises*, fully concentrate on that cosmic energy. Mentally open your medulla oblongata (the "mouth of God"), devotionally feeling that you are receiving the downward flow of "the ever-ready-to-help grace of God."

And before you practice, start with Yogananda's own words, which will inspire your cooperation with grace:

"I live, move, and have my being in Spirit,
as a fish lives in the water, and a bird in the air.
I will consciously draw strength, health, and happiness
from this all-enveloping Presence."†

2) *Hong-Sau*: the spiritual eye as a door to grace

Every time you meditate using the *Hong-Sau* technique, you are already practicing cooperation with grace. In fact, to receive grace, Yogananda states that "the right spirit is an attitude of unconditional love for God. The right place is within yourself. The right way is in the silence of deep meditation."‡

Especially effective is the advanced version of the *Hong-Sau* technique, in which the breath is visualized entering and exiting through the spiritual eye. Swami Kriyananda explains: "Spiritual aspirants should concentrate their gaze and attention from the beginning at that point. Thus, they will hasten the coming of ecstasy's dawn. This practice will enable them to cooperate with the natural flow of divine grace."§

---

* *The Art and Science of Raja Yoga* † *East-West*, October 1933 ‡ *The Essence of Self-Realization*
§ *Rays of the Same Light*

3) Kriya Yoga: flowing with grace

Kriya Yoga (Yogananda's highest technique of meditation) is the technique *par excellence* for cooperating with grace, if it is practiced with love. The full technique cannot be described here, because it is given only in a special initiation ceremony. However, what is important is that, during his practice, the Kriya Yogi first offers himself upward into God's light, cooperating with His ascending current of grace before receiving His blessings through the downward current of grace. Kriya Yoga could, in fact, perfectly well be called *Kripa Yoga*, "the yoga of grace", as it helps us to fully enter into the flow of God's grace.

Yogananda describes this inner experience of grace as follows: "Feel the Spirit of God on the altar of the spine, for the spine is the altar of God, and there you must feel the glory of the universe... Your whole center of consciousness is in the spine, and the sensation of the spine when awakened is indescribable. That is where your heaven is. Your whole mind will never be concentrated on anything else but that... In order to know the soul, you must concentrate on the spine. Yoga tells you the science of life. Behind this engine room of the body is God. Behind the spinal centers [chakras] is God. If you concentrate there, you will find Him."*

The rivers flowing in *iḍa* and *pingala* (through the "spinal shrines" of the chakras) can, in fact, be felt as sacred energies, the energy of God's grace. In his Master's ashram, Yogananda used to sing a chant which describes this sacred aspect of the inner currents:

> "For thy weal's (welfare's) sake,
> all-pervading God flows
> as *iḍa*, then *pingala*,
> whenever thy breath blows.
> On the left, good *iḍa*,
> on the right *pingala* river.
> "In the middle ever flows *sushumna*,
> Cosmic Redeemer.""

---

* Patanjali Lessons

If you are not a Kriya Yogi, during your practice of pranayama and meditation, try to experience the dual flow of grace which Swami Kriyananda describes in these words: "Gradually, with the increase of devotional magnetism, God's grace is attracted, to *descend* into human consciousness. The soul, soaring *upward* on rays of heavenly grace, passes through the portals of the spiritual eye and out into the infinite freedom of Spirit."*

You can get a taste of it by practicing the *Hong-Sau* version in which one visualizes energy going up the spine with the inhalation and down the spine with the exhalation. This practice is called, as we said, "Baby-Kriya," and you can use it to feel the dual currents in the spine so that you are already cooperating with grace.

Other mystical traditions also work with that same dual flow of grace. Kriyananda explains this fascinating fact: "Kriya Yoga is a particular kind of action or technique that draws on universal, central and, to some extent, commonly known facts of human nature. The Christian *Hesychasts* of Greece, centuries ago, drew on these facts when they counseled that the recitation of the well-known prayer, 'Lord Jesus Christ have mercy on us,' should be uttered in conjunction with the breath. The first three words, they said, should be uttered while inhaling, and the next four, 'have mercy on us,' while exhaling. The first part of the formula is an appeal. It is, therefore, offered up to Christ and to the superconscious with the *upward-flowing* energy. The last part is a request to receive grace into the body and into one's self. It, therefore, accompanies the downward-flowing energy with exhalation, seeking to *bring grace down* to oneself."†

4) Ananda Yoga: grace-stimulating asanas

Also try Ananda Yoga, which is an enlightened form of Hatha Yoga, as it comes from teachers who lived in grace themselves.

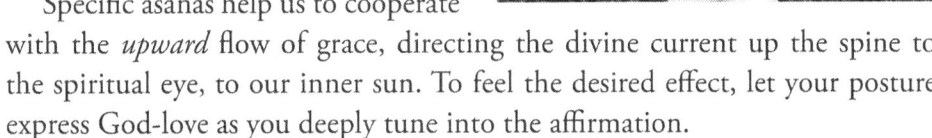

Specific asanas help us to cooperate with the *upward* flow of grace, directing the divine current up the spine to the spiritual eye, to our inner sun. To feel the desired effect, let your posture express God-love as you deeply tune into the affirmation.

* *Rays of the Same Light*
† *God Is For Everyone*

◑ **SETU BANDHASANA** (*Bridge Pose*). Affirm: "I offer every thought as a bridge to divine grace."

◐ **PARSVOTANASANA** (*Side-stretching Pose*). Affirm: "I offer myself fully into the flow of grace."

◑ **SARVANGASANA** (*Shoulderstand*). Affirm: "God's peace now floods my being."

This effort to direct our life-force upward is actually one of the main purposes of the yoga postures. Swami Kriyananda explains: "The general aim of Hatha Yoga is to use the body to *push*, or gently *nudge*, the energy upward toward the brain."* How to do that properly is important, but is not central to our discussion here.

Other Ananda Yoga asanas help us to cooperate with the *downward* flow of grace, from God into us. Again, to experience this, fill the posture with your heart's devotion, as you concentrate on the inner experience of the affirmations:

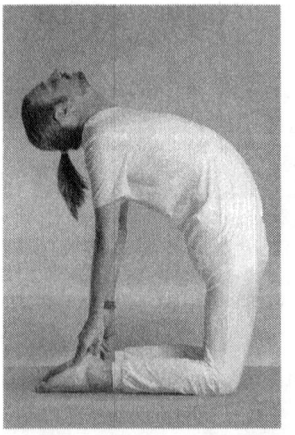

◐ **USTRASANA** (*Camel Pose*). Affirm: "With calm faith, I open to Thy Light."

◑ **TRIKONASANA** (*Triangle Pose*). Affirm: "Energy and joy flood my body cells! Joy descends to me!"

* *The Art and Science of Raja Yoga*

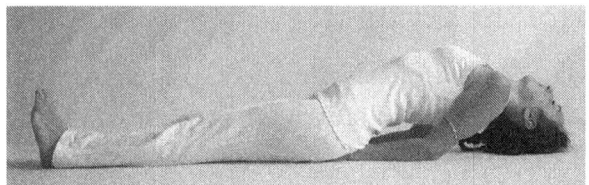

◐ **MATSYASANA** (*Fish Pose*). Affirm: **"My soul floats on waves of cosmic light."** Swami Kriyananda specifies for Matsyasana: "One should feel that he is floating on waves of Cosmic Light, completely submissive to the ebb and flow of divine grace."*

This is the highest form of asana practice according to him: "The highest purpose of yoga is simply to place oneself in a position to receive fully a *downpouring* of Spirit. If God's grace is not experienced in the average human life, it is not because of divine indifference, but because man's energies and attention are diverted elsewhere."†

Through the centuries, the ancient Indian Scriptures have encouraged this grace-inviting attitude. Famously, the *Hatha Yoga Pradipika* (15th century) counsels: "In a clean spot, clean room and charming ground, [the yogi] should spread a soft asana [cloth to sit on]. Having seated himself on it, let him remember in his mind his Guru and his God. Having extolled the place and the time, let him take up the vow thus: 'Today by the grace of God, I will perform pranayama with asana for gaining *samadhi* and its fruits.' He should salute the Infinite Deva, Lord of the *Nagas*, to ensure success in the asanas."

This is not some old-fashioned teaching. It is timeless wisdom. In fact, every sincere modern Hatha Yogi should start his session in this spirit: "Let my yoga be cooperation with grace."

5) Chanting: making grace shine brightly

Most importantly, *all* of the above techniques must be permeated with love for God, if we want to receive the light of grace. Techniques take us to the skylight, but it's our devotion which opens the curtains. Chanting stimulates that opening process. Yogananda, as we have seen, specifically promises that his Cosmic Chants "will bring God-communion and ecstatic joy, and through these the healing of body, mind, and soul." And Kriyananda clarifies: "What Yogananda's method of chanting accomplishes is to awaken in the mind the thought 'In these ways I will cooperate with His grace.'"‡

* *The Art and Science of Raja Yoga*
† *Ibid*
‡ *Awaken to Superconsciousness*

Go for the skylight!

So during this next week, when we sit in meditation, let's go straight to the skylight of our inner house and open wide the curtains. As we progress, the promise is that we will even learn how to exit the house (ego-consciousness) altogether. The exit door is the skylight. Then we shall enjoy the full splendor of the sun, play in it and live as God intended us to be: entertained, joyfully free and forever basking in the light of His grace.

Rise NOW!

Let's not wait for that glorious moment to come in the future, but rather let's experience this state of grace here and now. Sit up, practice some *Hong-Sau*, and then, sitting in silence, look upward toward your inner skylight. Visualize yourself already receiving the bright light of grace as it flows through you as the vibration of OM, the Holy Ghost or Divine Mother, and purifies you completely. To deepen this state, contemplate one of Yogananda's *Whispers From Eternity*.

SATISFY MY SOUL-HUNGER

O All-Pervading Spirit,
the breeze of Thy inspiration
has removed every cloud from my heart.
The firmament of my mind is now clear.
Purified, I behold only Thee, everywhere.
The sunshine of Thy joy spreads rapidly
to the farthest shores of my being.
After long ages of hunger,
I feed on Thy light.
By Thy grace,
and by my constant
wakefulness in Thee,
may this joy be mine
forever, forever, and forever!

WEEK 3 OF SELF-REALIZATION TRAINING: COOPERATING WITH GRACE

Follow this sequence each day:

1) Practice the 20 *body-part recharging*, following the instructions on cooperating with grace in this chapter.

2) Optionally practice the yoga asanas. Use mainly the postures mentioned above, practicing cooperation with grace.

3) Practice chanting as a way to cooperate with grace.

4) Then follow the standard sequence of the *Hong-Sau* technique (Week 4 of Meditation Training), practicing *Hong-Sau* in the spine or in the spiritual eye. Use one of the suggestions described in Week 1 of Self-Realization Training. Again **practice cooperation with grace**.

5) As you practice the second phase without the *Hong-Sau* mantra, looking intensely upward, feel again that you are **opening up to grace**.

6) Your second training concerns daily life: practice **keeping the sense of grace** within you during the day.

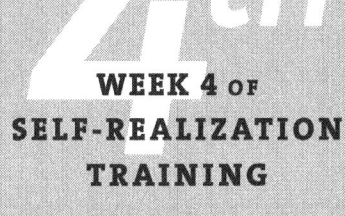

WEEK 4 OF SELF-REALIZATION TRAINING

The Spiritual Eye

"During deep meditation, the single or spiritual eye becomes visible within the central part of the forehead. This omniscient eye is variously referred to in scriptures as the third eye, the star of the East, the inner eye, the dove descending from heaven, the eye of Shiva, the eye of intuition, etc."

Autobiography of a Yogi

The inner eye of heaven

We have an extremely important focus this week, the importance of which cannot be over-estimated for our meditations and our inner evolution. It will greatly elevate our meditative efforts and consists of concentrated focus on the spiritual eye.

> *The* SECRET *of* MEDITATION *is...*
>
> to focus your gaze and attention at the Christ Center between the eyebrows — the seat of ecstasy in the body.

The position of the eyes during *Hong-Sau*

When describing the *Hong-Sau* technique in his Praecepta Lessons, Yogananda writes: "You must get used to the practicing of this technique with your eyes gently concentrated upon the point between the eyebrows. Do not strain the eyes. However, if you are not used to holding the eyes in this position, practice some of the time with your eyes half open, but most of the time with eyes closed. You can practice with eyes closed, and in leisure hours lie down on your back, and watch the breath, mentally chanting *Hong-Sau*. The more you practice in your leisure hours, the greater will be the results. Work overtime and you will gain still better results."

The seat of Christ Consciousness

Every time we concentrate at the point between the eyebrows, we stimulate our contact with superconsciousness, raising our awareness. This is why in pictures we often see saints looking up. Yogananda also called the spiritual eye the seat of Christ Consciousness. It is of enormous importance if we want to approach the higher states of meditation. Give it your full attention this week.

Yogananda describes in his *Autobiography* how persistent practice with the spiritual eye finally helps us to perceive the one light behind all matter: "Long

concentration on the liberating spiritual eye has enabled the yogi to destroy all illusions concerning matter and its gravitational weight; thenceforth he sees the universe as an essentially undifferentiated mass of light."

In deep and calm meditation, the "omniscient eye" appears in the forehead as a golden circle surrounding a blue field with a white five-pointed star in the middle. At an earlier stage, one may see a light, or various colors.

It is the door to the inner paradise. "Paradise" in fact is generally thought of as somewhere up in the sky. In truth it is a state of consciousness which all of us can enter when we center our energy and our awareness in the spiritual eye.

Haven't we all have had moments of paradise? Moments when a ray of heaven, from the spiritual eye, touched our consciousness and old ways of behaving ceased, at least for that moment?

Yogis teach us how to consciously "knock at heaven's door," at the spiritual eye: through deep concentration, lifting our gaze, looking at whatever appears in the forehead. This gives new meaning to the Biblical counsel: "Knock, and it shall be opened unto you."*

Jesus described a mystical effect when one advances in the technique of gazing into the luminous spiritual eye: "If therefore thine eye be single, thy whole body shall be full of light."†

Inspiring pictures

There are precious pictures of the Masters of Kriya Yoga—Yogananda, Sri Yukteswar, Lahiri Mahasaya and Mahavatar Babaji – which show them with half-open eyes, gazing intently at the spiritual eye. During the following days, as you focus on that same inner point, it might be helpful to find one of these photos on the internet, print it, and place it where you meditate.

Babaji-Krishna

* Matthew 7:7
† Matthew 6:22

The Spiritual Eye / 191

Shambhavi Mudra

In classical Yoga Scriptures, the technique of lifting the eyes and gazing intently inward, at the point between the eyebrows is of enormous importance. It is called *Shambhavi Mudra*, the "Mudra of Shiva," and is described as the highest and most important of all *mudras* (seals). To see how to practice it, go to YouTube and search for "Yogananda on Sleep," and watch at the end of the film how Yogananda lifts his eyes, as he consciously enters superconscious bliss: that is true *Shambhavi Mudra*.

In the *Autobiography of a Yogi*, Lahiri Mahasaya refers to Shambhavi Mudra in a handwritten letter in Bengali script. Translated, it reads: "He who has attained a state of calmness wherein his eyelids do not blink, has achieved Sambhabi Mudra."

In the same book we read how Yogananda taught this technique already to the children in his school: "It is no novelty at Ranchi to see an appealing little figure, aged nine or ten years, sitting for an hour or more in unbroken poise, the unwinking gaze directed to the spiritual eye."

Swami Kriyananda explains its essential importance for all of us: "The spiritual eye is as much a part of every human being as the brain. It is *more* a reality than the body parts, the loss or amputation of which cannot affect man essentially. The light of the spiritual eye can never be separated from our inner reality, for the simple reason that *we are* that reality. Even when we lose the body at death, we retain this inner light, *for it is of the soul*."*

Colors, angels... but we are as blind as a bat

Yogananda explains: "If you could see with your spiritual eye you would see a rainbow of colors. The color scheme is so beautiful in the astral world. This world is ugly here, and a million angels are passing here right now and you don't see them. We are all as *blind as a bat*. Because our eyes have been spoiled by gross light."†

The Scriptures have taught for millennia that daylight is darkness for the yogi as compared to the inner light; like a little candle compared to the bright sun. The Bhagavad Gita states this clearly (2:69): "That which is night for the unenlightened is day for the yogi. And that which is day for ordinary people is night for the yogi-seer (who perceives the inner reality)."

* *Rays Of the One Light*
† Patanjali Lessons

That intense inner brightness is also mentioned in the Bible: "And they shall see his face; and his name shall be *in their foreheads*. And there shall be no night there; and they need no candle, neither light of the sun; for *the Lord God giveth them light*: and they shall reign for ever and ever."*

Such scriptural passages are sometimes hard to grasp. Yogananda enlightens us: "This light you see is the darkness. The greatest thing is this, that our sixth sense is the spiritual eye. The seat of the spiritual eye is right here between the two eyes. That is the eye that has not been opened. When you develop you can keep that eye open. It is like a tunnel, you can see through it."†

The spiritual eye becomes a tunnel, which leads into the colorful *astral* world (of energy), then into the higher *causal* world (of thought), and finally into the blissful kingdom of God (beyond vibration and creation).

Enough of being human chicks!

Few perhaps have defined the spiritual eye in Yogananda's colorful way: "The meaning of the spiritual eye is this: when a chick is in the egg shell, its whole world is the egg shell. It doesn't know any other world. When it breaks through the shell it comes into another world. So *we are human chicks*! We don't know what is beyond. But through the spiritual eye we see the astral world. There marvelous currents and lights are floating about. Through the two eyes we see the world and through the spiritual eye we can perceive the astral world. That is why Jesus said, 'Seeing, ye see not.' The Gita says, 'Concentrate on the center between the eyes.' You will notice pictures of Jesus and all saints show them looking up in that spiritual light."‡

Practice

All the above quotes are not really meant to instruct and explain, but only to inspire us, to instill us with the enthusiasm, with the longing to practice with our spiritual eye.

And how do we do that? Just by gazing there? Yes, but there are also some practical methods for sharpening our inner gaze. Below you can find three effective techniques to experiment with.

* *Revelations* 22: 4–5
† Patanjali Lessons
‡ Ibid

1) A technique for developing a steady gaze: *Tratak*

The first is a technique for developing an unblinking steady gaze. Yogananda in fact tells us: "Restless and constantly blinking eyes indicate a restless mind; quiet, *unblinking eyes*, a calm mind. God is not visible, not recognizable to the ordinary restless eyes of mortal man. But fixing the eyes at one point induces the mind to grow calm and concentrated."

Fixing the eyes on one point is a classical yoga practice called *tratak*. It consists of gazing at an object, often a candle, which is placed a little higher than the eyes and at a short distance from them. Stare at that object, never looking away, keeping your gaze steady, *unblinking*, even if the eyes fill with tears.

Yogananda taught a fun form of *tratak*. He invented a device, calling it the "Temple of Silence," which was fixed on the head, rather like earmuffs. Attached to it was a manufactured spiritual eye, which hung a short distance in front of the eyes and served to focus the gaze. A marvelous invention for training us in a creative way to enter the "seat of ecstasy" in the body, the "Christ Center"—the Kutastha, as it is called in India, which means "the unchangeable."

2) A technique for higher concentration: visualization

Visualization is a powerful technique to develop inner concentration. It even leads to the *siddhi* (power) of materialization. Yogananda explained that he was able to keep looking at a room and concentrating upon it until, when he closed his eyes, he could still see the room exactly as it was. This, he says, is the *first step in deep concentration*, but adds that most people haven't the patience to practice it. But he *did* have the patience. By continuing to practice visualization, as Yogananda points out, we will find that our thoughts become materialized. The cosmic law will so arrange it that whatsoever we are thinking of will be produced in actuality, if we command it to be so. He gives an example: if we think of an apple, and the apple appears in our hand, that would be a demonstration of the highest power of concentration."*

* *Man's Eternal Quest*, by Paramhansa Yogananda. "The Dream Nature of the World"

Try it. Experiment with it. Practice it. Intensely look at an apple (or any object in your room) for some time. Imprint the image in your mind. Then close your eyes. Looking at the point between the eyebrows, inwardly try to see that object as clearly as you can. You are strongly stimulating your spiritual eye.

3) A technique for gazing at the spiritual eye

There is another technique for stimulating our vision of the spiritual eye by using an external light, for example, a lamp. Yogananda says: "Look at a light and close your eyes. Forget the darkness around you and watch the blood red color within your eyelids. Try to *look intently* into that violet red color before you. Meditate on it and imagine that it is becoming bigger and bigger. Behold around you a dimly shining sea of violet light. You are a wave of light, a ripple of peace floating on the surface of the sea."*

When to focus on the spiritual eye during meditation

When you meditate, there is a correct moment for gazing intently at the spiritual eye. During *any* of Yogananda's techniques, the eyes are *always* turned upward to the spiritual eye, though the concentration is *not* focused there, but on the technique itself:

- While practicing *Hong Sau*, the eyes are focused at the spiritual eye while we concentrate on the breath and the mantra.

- During Kriya Yoga, the eyes are focused at the spiritual eye while we concentrate on the inner currents.

- During the OM-Technique, the eyes are focused at the spiritual eye while we focus on the inner sounds.

- During the *energization exercises*, the eyes are focused at the spiritual eye while we focus on directing energy in the body.

* *Metaphysical Meditations*

Hong-Sau

During our *Hong-Sau* meditation, the correct time for fully concentrating on the spiritual eye comes *after* the technique, when we abandon the mantra, during the last part of the meditation. At that moment we fix our gaze one-pointedly and with devotion at the "Christ Center," looking toward God. Let nothing take your concentration away from your spiritual eye. Penetrate the darkness with the arrow of concentration. It is the focused gaze of the saints.

Some practical guidelines

- Practice **daily** gazing with concentration at the spiritual eye. Make it one of the priorities of your sadhana.

- Practice in a **dark room**. Then the inner light is seen more easily.

- When you see the inner light, don't get excited. **Remain calm** and receive it with love.

- Try not to practice with the expectation of seeing the light. Expectation creates tension and frustration. Whatever comes, let it come. If the light doesn't come, know that just by concentrating on the spiritual eye you have stimulated a higher consciousness which will bear marvelous results in your daily life.

During the day

All through the day, look up at the spiritual eye as often as you can remember to do so. Yogananda called this practice one of the most powerful techniques for our inner spiritual evolution. Try it!

Balance

However, there is an important *caveat*, as explained by Swami Kriyananda: "The Master told us that when he first came to Sri Yukteswar's ashram, he would keep his mind and gaze focused at the point between the eyebrows as much as possible. 'If you want to make very rapid progress on the spiritual path,' he used to tell us, 'keep your mind always centered there.' This practice must be joined to, however, and supported by the heart's devotion. For concentration at the spiritual eye, which is known as the *ajna chakra*, develops great will power, but it can also make one *ruthless* if it isn't combined with the heart's love. When will power is combined with love, great joy is the consequence."*

* *Conversations with Yogananda*

An affirmation

As you deepen your inner gaze, affirm with Yogananda:

"I will leave my finite mansion for my Infinite Mansion through the tunnel of the spiritual eye and breathlessness."

Yoga asanas

If you practice the postures, keep your inner gaze at the spiritual eye. Focus particularly on ⊂ **PARVATASANA** (*Seated Mountain Pose*), which pushes the energy up to the spiritual eye. Once you are in the pose, inhale with the diaphragm, hold the breath and pull the abdomen in, directing the air and energy upward. Affirm: **"My thoughts and energy rise up to touch the sky."**

Also all the inverted postures bring the energy to the spiritual eye. Practice them with that specific purpose in mind:

⊂ **HALASANA** (*Plow Pose*)

⊃ **SARVANGASANA** (*Shoulderstand*)

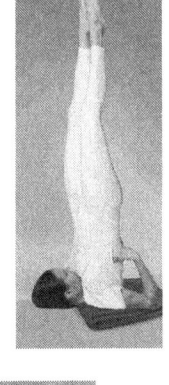

⊂ **SIRSHASANA** (*Headstand*)

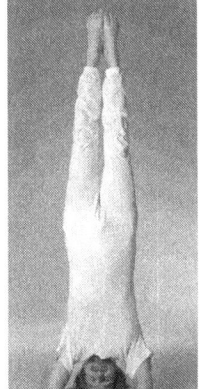

⊍ **VIPARITA KARANI** (*Simple Inverted Pose*)

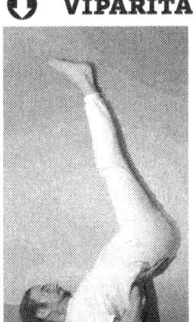

⊃ **PINCHA MAYURASANA** (*Peacock Feather Pose*)

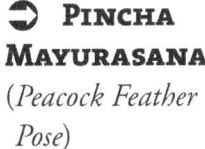

The Spiritual Eye

WEEK 4 OF SELF-REALIZATION TRAINING:
THE SPIRITUAL EYE

Follow this sequence each day:

1) Practice the 20 *body-part recharging*. Keep your gaze at the spiritual eye.

2) Optionally practice the yoga asanas. Focus on bringing the energy to the spiritual eye. Use especially *Parvatasana* (Seated Mountain Pose) and the inverted postures.

3) Practice *tratak* and the other techniques described above.

4) Then follow the standard sequence of the *Hong-Sau* technique (Week 4 of Meditation Training), practicing *Hong-Sau* in the spine or in the spiritual eye. Apply one of the suggestions described in Week 1 of Self-realization Training. **Keep your eyes always lifted.**

5) Your training is especially to be practiced during the last phase: **intensely gaze into the spiritual eye**. Feel you are going toward infinity.

6) Your second training concerns your daily life: **look upward to the spiritual eye** as often as you can remember to do so.

WEEK 5 OF SELF-REALIZATION TRAINING

Attunement

"The characteristic features of Indian culture have long been a search for ultimate verities and the concomitant disciple-guru relationship."

Autobiography of a Yogi

The "extra help" of a saint

Saint Teresa of Avila

Do you enjoy diamonds? Then this is a special week for you as we will explore how to "wear" the diamond of spiritual life: how to open up to a true guru.

The word *guru* means "dispeller of darkness"—he who turns darkness into light. Once Swami Kriyananda was asked in an interview: "Do we need a guru?" His answer was simple: "No, we don't." But then he added with a smile: "However, if your goal in life is to reach Self-realization, if you want to find God, then yes, you do need a guru."

Why is this? The answer is that our own darkness simply has too many layers. It is impossible to overcome them all by ourselves. The ego can't overcome the ego. We need another light to shine in us in order to dispel the darkness. The guru is that light. He is like a brilliant diamond which we invite into our being.

Self-realization means transforming our "inner iron" into "gold," our darkness into light, our imperfection into perfection, our mortality into immortality. Without the help of a spiritual "philosopher's stone," this process of complete transformation is impossible as the great yogis teach. For millennia, therefore, they have insisted on the need for a guru, or enlightened teacher.

Centuries ago, the famous Adi Shankaracharya wrote in his *Century of Verses*: "There is no known comparison in all the three worlds [causal, astral, material] for the venerable guru that bestows knowledge. If the philosopher's stone be assumed as such, it only turns iron into gold, but, alas! cannot convert it into philosopher's stone. The venerable teacher, on the other hand, creates equality with himself in the disciple who takes refuge at his feet. He is therefore peerless, nay, even transcendental."

In short: without keeping the diamond of a saintly soul in our heart, our meditative life will never be as sparkling as it could be. Our own efforts alone do not suffice to fully unfold the glory of our soul and to plumb the depth of Spirit. For such advanced goals we need the presence of a saint whom we keep in our heart and mind.

> *The* **SECRET** *of* **MEDITATION** *is...*
>
> dwelling on the thought of great saints,
> past and present, who have known God;
> attuning your consciousness to theirs.

During this week, then, as we practice *Hong-Sau*, we will explore how to "wear" the diamond of a saintly soul during our meditations, practicing at his/her side.

Whom to choose?

Which saint should we choose? Of course, disciples of any Master already know their diamond. Otherwise, Swami Kriyananda in his "Secret of Meditation" cited above tells us that we can chose *any* saint, past or present. In other words, he can be in his body or not. You can choose freely, letting your heart decide.

The most important thing is to treat this saint as a precious diamond for your spiritual life: with love, care, and attention.

How to "wear" the diamond

Here is this week's plan for making our diamond shine brightly.

1) Prayer to the saint

When you sit down for your meditation, pray to the saint. Invite him. Great saints are gentlemen, they don't intrude without an invitation. You may use these words:

> "Beloved... *(name of saint)*,
>   I will enjoy you.
>   I will feel you in my emotions.
>   I will think you in my thoughts.
>   I will use your wisdom-guided will
>   to guide my habit-guided will."*

---

* *East-West* Magazine, 1932

Those on the path of Self-realization may choose the following prayer of Yogananda before beginning the *Hong-Sau* technique:

"Heavenly Father, Jesus Christ,
saints of all religions,
the Spirit in my body temple,
supreme master minds of India,
supreme master Babaji,
great master Lahiri Mahasaya,
master Swami Sri Yukteswar Giriji,
and Guru-Preceptor,
I bow to you all.
Lead me from ignorance to wisdom;
from restlessness to peace;
from desires to contentment."

2) Singing to the saint

Then sing to the saint. You can sing along to one of Yogananda's chants here: www.crystalclarity.com/TMOY_links

Dawn chant
Night has flown, dawn has come,
Wake my children wake! |:2
Sitting in the *asana* of meditation, |:2
Think ye of thy guru's lotus feet. |:2

Or you may choose a traditional Sanskrit chant, the *Guru Stotram*, followed by the "Hymn to Brahma": You can find both online at this link: www.crystalclarity.com/TMOY_links

The Meditation of Yogananda / 202

Guru Stotram

Gurur-Brahma, Gurur-Vishnu,
Gurur-Devo Maheshwara,
Guru-sakshat Para-Brahma,
tasmai Shri Gurave namah.

Brahmanandam parama sukhadam
kevalam gyana murtim,
dandva thitam gagana sadrisham
Tatvamsya di lakshyam,
ekam nityam, bimalam achalam,
sarvadhee sakshi bhutam,
bhava titam, triguna rahitam,
Sat-gurum tam namami.

Brahma, Vishnu, Shiva

The first verse means: "The guru is the creator (*Brahma*), the preserver (*Vishnu*), the destroyer (*Maheshwara, Shiva*); the guru is truly the transcendent divine. To him I bow."

The second part can be chanted in English in this way:

Full of God's bliss, in joy of the heavens,
your wisdom is cosmic and pure,
most high you are in your limitless vision,
settled in the "I am That."

One with the Lord,
eternal, unmoving,
the everlasting seer of all,
Far, far beyond any guna and thought,
Sat-Guru, I bow to you.

Whatever chant you choose, fill it with your heart. Love is the most effective method of attunement.

3) Meditating with the saint

When you start your meditation, try to feel your saint close, letting his vibrations magnetically infuse yours. There are various ways to do this:

- Feel that he is sitting inside your body and that he is practicing the *Hong-Sau* technique through you.

- You may visualize him meditating at your side. Feel him alive, present, intimately near. Yogananda sang these words: "Sitting in the silence on the sunny banks of my mind, sitting in the silence, with my guru by my side…"

- Or, if you prefer, visualize him in front of you, looking at you with love and power. Alternatively, you may imagine that you are sitting inside your saint: he is your aura, your shakti. Or imagine that you are not even there but that his body alone is meditating.

- Or feel his presence in your heart, following another one of Yogananda's songs: "Think ye in thy heart, lotus feet of thy guru."

- Swami Kriyananda also practiced another technique: he visualized Yogananda sitting in miniature form on the top of his head.

- Alternatively, "If you have a guru, you may also think of him thus. Visualize that spirit descending through your medulla, brain, and spine and out into your nervous system, filling your entire body. Feel that he has, in some mysterious but exalted sense, become you. And feel divine devotion toward him, especially in your heart. You are that divine consciousness which now dwells in your body! Pray that it fill you and purify you of every human imperfection. Raise the attunement you feel in your heart and offer it up to God."*

Experiment and find out which visualization is most effective for you. Practice your techniques with *his* power, with *his* concentration, with *his* devotion. See if this kind of attunement gives a new brilliance to your meditations.

In all the above practices, mentally ask, "How should I be doing this? Show me." If you ask questions inwardly with attunement, you'll find that the answers will be forthcoming.

* *The Hindu Way of Awakening*

Such a practice gradually changes our magnetism: "One can develop cosmic magnetism by thinking of God and saintly people. By concentrating deeply upon a certain personality, one can attract that personality. That is why one should think only of great individuals."*

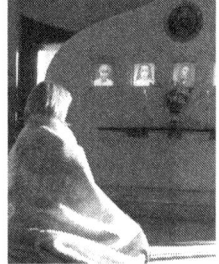

4) A Technique of Attunement

You may also include the following technique, which will help you to attune to your saint:

"To tune in to the guru's consciousness, visualize him in the spiritual eye. Mentally call to him there. Imagine his eyes, especially, gazing at you. Invite his consciousness to inspire your own. Then, after calling to him for some time, try to feel his response in your heart. The heart is the center of intuition in the body. It is your 'radio-receiver.' Your 'broadcasting station' is situated in the Christ center between the eyebrows. It is from this center that your will broadcasts into the universe your thoughts and ideas. Once you feel an answer in the heart, call to the guru deeply, 'Introduce me to God.'" †

Becoming the diamond

What happens if we progress with our attunement? We increasingly absorb the brilliancy of the diamond and gradually become a spiritual diamond ourselves. Here is a little story to illustrate this point:

"There was a devotee sitting before an image of his Guru, chanting and tossing flowers onto it as an expression of his devotion. His concentration became so deep that, all at once, he beheld the whole universe contained within his consciousness. 'Ah!' he cried, 'I have been putting flowers on another's image, but now I see that I, untouched by this body, am the Sustainer of the universe. I bow to my Self!' And he began throwing the flowers onto his own head."‡

Yoga asanas

Use **VIRABHADRASANA 1** (*Warrior* 1) to practice attunement with a saint. Open your arms as if you were receiving great power from him or her. Affirm: **"I attune my will to the Source of all power."**

* *Inner Culture*, July 1941
† *The Essence of Self-Realization*
‡ *Ibid*

WEEK 5 OF SELF-REALIZATION TRAINING: ATTUNEMENT

Follow this sequence each day:

1) Practice the 20 *body-part recharging*. Mentally keep a saint by your side.

2) Optionally practice the yoga asanas. Focus especially on *Virabhadrasana* 1 (Warrior 1).

3) Then follow the standard sequence of the *Hong-Sau* technique (Week 4 of Meditation Training), practicing *Hong-Sau* in the spine or in the spiritual eye. Follow one of the suggestions described in Week 1 of Self-realization Training. Always **meditate with the saint of your choice**. Daily practice one the techniques described above.

4) During the second phase look upward. Offer yourself into infinity. Absorb yourself in whatever soul perception comes to you.

5) Your second training concerns daily life: **keep the saint by your side** as much as you can.

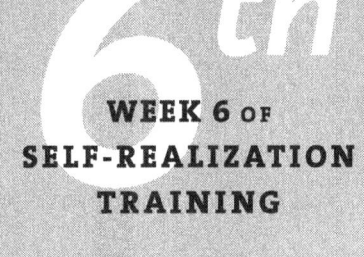

Space

WEEK 6 OF SELF-REALIZATION TRAINING

"Closing my eyes,
I saw flashes of lightning; the vast space within me was a chamber of molten light. I opened my eyes and observed the same dazzling radiance. The room became a part of that infinite vault which I beheld with interior vision."

Autobiography of a Yogi

A journey into space

One of Swami Kriyananda's *Secrets of Meditation* deserves special attention, because it offers great inspiration for our meditations:

> The **SECRET** of **MEDITATION** is...
>
> to feel space in the body,
> and gradually expand that feeling
> from the body outward,
> into infinite space.

This week, our aim in our meditations is to experience this expansion into space, thus giving a new color to our daily *Hong-Sau* technique. Like curious meditative scientists, let's experiment and see whether it improves our experience.

In your place of meditation

To tune into the topic of space during this week, it might help you to find a beautiful photo of the cosmos or the galaxy on the internet and to print it. Place it where you meditate, as a reminder of the vastness of space.

As a space shuttle: an inspiration

When starting your meditation, before practicing the techniques, contemplate the following passage from the *Autobiography of a Yogi*, in which Yogananda describes his inner journey into **space**:

> "A swelling glory within me began to envelop towns, continents, the earth, solar, and stellar systems, tenuous nebulae, and floating universes. The entire cosmos, gently luminous, like a city seen afar at night, glimmered within the infinitude of my being. The sharply etched global outlines faded somewhat at the farthest edges; there I could see a mellow radiance, ever-undiminished. It was indescribably subtle; the planetary pictures were formed of a grosser light."

A space pranayama before *Hong-Sau*

Then practice this pranayama: "Sit upright, away from the back of your chair (unless you are sitting on the floor). Concentrate in the spine. Remember, the spine is not your backbone (those protrusions that you feel along the back). It runs more or less through the center of your body. Feel that *as your* center. Sway the body left and right. Feel a resistance to that movement in the spine—as though you were perfectly still at your own center.

Now, feel yourself breathing *in the spine*: up with every inhalation, down with every exhalation. Let the movement begin in the region of the heart, starting at a point slightly below it and extending slightly above.

Lengthen the flow gradually, beginning lower in the spine and ending higher up.

Lastly, take a slow, deep breath through the nostrils, beginning at the base of the spine and ending at the point between the eyebrows. Hold the breath at that point as long as it is comfortable to do so.

This time, with your exhalation, feel your breath and consciousness soaring out through the forehead, taking you with them into infinite space.

Concentrate, now, on infinity. Feel that from your own center all things are cognizable."*

Space during the *Hong-Sau* technique

Then start your *Hong-Sau* practice. Usually we follow Yogananda's teachings; namely, to observe the breath, as if it were the breath of another person, thereby *dis-identifying* with it, as he teaches that "by watching the breath, you metaphysically destroy the identification of the soul with the breath and the body."

However, one can also do the exact opposite, obtaining optimal results: to *identify* with the breath, not with its physical aspect and function, but with its spiritual aspect of space. Swami Kriyananda explains it like this:

"By concentration on the breath one acquires the consciousness of being air, or infinite space.... When concentrating on the breath, keep your mind focused not so much on the mechanism of breathing (the movement of the navel, lungs, etc.) as on the breath itself. In this way, your mental identification will become at last with air, with space, not with a merely negative cessation of physical movement.

Direct the will, rather, toward the thought of *becoming* the air that is flowing in the nose, or of becoming boundless space at the Christ center. Meditate on space, and on the feeling of freedom from body-awareness."†

* *Awaken to Superconsciousness*
† *The Art and Science of Raja Yoga*

Space when the breath is still

In moments when, during your *Hong-Sau* practice, the breath becomes very still, try this: "As your practice deepens particularly enjoy the pauses when the breath is not flowing; use them to become more fully identified with the thought: 'I am He! I am infinite space!'"*

Space at the end of meditation

After your *Hong-Sau* practice, listen to this visualization which you find here: www.crystalclarity.com/TMOY_links

> Sit upright. Sit very still.
> Feel that, surrounding your body,
> Is an infinity of dark **space**.
> Listen intently:
> Listen to the whispering silence!
>
> Out of silence was sound born.
> Out of darkness the light came.
> Of that light, suns and galaxies drew their substance.
> Light, not form, is the truth that infuses the universe.
>
> Surround your body now with a halo of blue light—
> Soft, soothing—a luminous peace.
> Light enters you;
> It pierces the pores of your skin;
> Space lies outside you no longer: It has made you its own.
> It reaches deep into your muscles, your bones.
> The sense of heaviness has been lifted from you.
> You are made of pure light.
>
> Like a boundless sphere, now,
> The light has started to grow.
> Shining freedom—claim it as your own!
> Light and joy thrill the air of the room.
> The people, the objects nearby—
> All these, in the peacefulness of that blue light and joy,
> Are one with you.

---

* *The Art and Science of Raja Yoga*

See: Light is embracing the house in which you live.
It reaches out to your neighborhood—to your township.

Like an expanding sail, ever outward
The light swells.
It embraces your country—Your continent—The world!
The whole world is basking
In the peaceful radiance of your joy.

Softly, now—
Release your light from the boundaries of this world.
Behold, light rays stream out
To the limits of the solar system—
To distant stars—to our galactic fringe.
At last, countless galaxies in all space,
Their stars, tiny like the lights of a far-off city,
Glimmer serenely in the vastness of your being.

God's light and you are one!
God's joy and you are one!
O ray of the Infinite!
You are not only this little body: You are more—much more.
Boundless! Eternal!
All the atoms of creation gather,
Like thirsty children,
To drink from the waters,
To play in the fountain spray
Of your inexhaustible peace!"*

An affirmation of space at the end of meditation

At the end of your meditation, repeat this *Metaphysical Meditation* by Yogananda:

"I soar in the plane of consciousness
　above, beneath, on the left, on the right,
　within and without, everywhere,
　to find that in every nook of my space-home
　I have always been in the sacred presence of my Father."

* *Awaken to Superconsciousness*

Yoga asanas to experience space

If you practice the postures, try to experiment with them in order to deepen your experience of space.

◐ **PADAHASTASANA** (*Jackknife Pose*)

When you are in the asana, be aware of the tensions that prevent you from stretching further. Release the tensions and in order to release them, think space at the points of stretch: "The yogi is taught, as an exercise in mental freedom, to meditate on vast space. Normally, such spatial awareness is obstructed by one's sense of physical heaviness. In *Padahastasana*, this natural sense of gravity is disoriented by the half-upward, half-downward, position of the body. If one can relax in this position, one finds that the conflicting directions help the mind to overcome its bondage to gravity. Affirm mentally, '**Nothing on earth can hold me.**'"*

◐ **MUKTASANA** (*Freedom Pose*)

Again enter the pose. "Feel the triumphant freedom that is suggested by this position. Feel your energy and consciousness being swept upward to the sky, into space. Affirm mentally: '**I am free! I am free!**'"†

◐ **SAVASANA** (*deep relaxation in space*)

Stretching out comfortably on the floor, allow Swami Kriyananda to guide you: "Think of your body as surrounded by space—space in all directions, spreading out to infinity.

"Now think of your feet, and visualize this space gradually seeping through the pores of the skin into your feet, until your feet become space. Visualize this space as gradually coming up into the calves, thighs, hips, the abdomen and stomach, the hands, forearms, upper arms, shoulders, chest, the back

* *The Art and Science of Raja Yoga*
† *Ibid*

of the neck, sides of the neck, the throat, jaw, tongue, lips, cheeks, eyes, and brain. In feeling space in your brain, release from your mind all regrets about the past, all worries about the future. Rest in the infinite ocean of the eternal Present. The objects of endless human concern no longer exist. There is nothing in all eternity, but the Right Here, the Right Now.

"Affirm mentally: **'Bones, muscles, movement I surrender now; anxiety, elation, and depression, churning thoughts: All these I give into the hands of peace.'**"*

Taking space into daily life

Try to take the happy feeling of expansion into your daily life. Every now and then, when your work allows it, open and close your eyes, remember your meditation and repeat:

> "With open eyes I behold myself as the little body.
> With closed eyes I perceive myself as the cosmic center
> around which revolves the sphere of eternity,
> the sphere of bliss, the sphere of omnipresent,
> omniscient, living space."†

---

* *The Art and Science of Raja Yoga*
† *Metaphysical Meditations*

WEEK 6 OF SELF-REALIZATION TRAINING: SPACE

Follow this sequence each day:

1) Practice the 20 *body-part recharging*.

2) Optionally practice the yoga asanas. Focus on *Padahastasana* (Jackknife Pose), *Muktasana* (Freedom Pose) and *Savasana* (Corpse Pose).

3) Then follow the standard sequence of the *Hong-Sau* technique (Week 4 of Meditation Training), practicing *Hong-Sau* in the spine or in the spiritual eye. Apply one of the suggestions described in Week 1 of Self-realization Training. Experiment with the practices explained for this week: the aim is to **experience space**.

4) During the second phase especially, without *Hong-Sau*, look upward and move into space.

WEEK 7 OF SELF-REALIZATION TRAINING

Freedom

"'Body' signifies any soul-encasement, whether gross or subtle. The three bodies [physical, astral, causal] are cages for the Bird of Paradise."

Autobiography of a Yogi

The mystery of suffering

Our soul—the essence of our being—consists of pure bliss (*Satchidananda*), as the great Masters teach us. But do you feel this bliss, right now? Probably not. Instead we all suffer, go through dificult times and live a life which can be amazingly tough. How can that be? It seems impossible, given our blissful nature.

The cause of our suffering is actually astounding: we simply don't know who we are, thinking that we are a tiny physical reality, while in truth we are a limitless being.

All our trouble is caused by that deep-seated identification with something we are not: the body, the mind, our personality, our feelings, our character. All this is called "ego," the little I, which Swami Kriyananda defines as a "bundle of self-definitions." Yogananda describes it as the "distorted soul," because, by identifying with the body, our soul (the true "I") becomes completely distorted.

The whole world, then, lives a distorted life, and the consequence is global: suffering.

The bird of paradise

There is a story of a magnificent colorful *bird of paradise* which, alas, one day was caught, put into a cage and placed outside a house. As it happened, there she laid an egg. But soon after her little chick was born, she died. The young *bird of paradise* grew up in that tiny cage, considering this life to be perfectly normal: after all, it was the only thing he had ever known. Nobody had even taught him how to fly. One bright day, however, another *bird of paradise* swooped down from heaven, saw him, and talked forcefully to him:

"Listen! You are a bird, born to glide freely through the sky. You are *not* meant to be in that cage." The younger bird was utterly surprised. "Really?" With great effort the older *bird of paradise* finally managed to open the door of the cage and the young one hopped out. "Fly," the older one cried, "look at me, imitate me." It took some time, but after much effort the young *bird of paradise* soared into the infinite sky. It was a joy never to be forgotten, a supreme liberation, an endless feeling of happiness. He had become himself again. He had found his true nature.

The Meditation of Yogananda / 216

You, the reader, will certainly have grasped the moral of the story: every one of us is just like that *bird of paradise*: majestic, free, colorful, but which finds itself locked in the little cage of a body. In Yogananda's words: "The *bird of paradise* has become the bird encaged behind the prison bars of flesh."*

The trouble is that for a long time we have had no idea that we are actually in a cage. The body felt (and feels) so normal, so much like "I." We look in the mirror and that's who we think we are.

We make the cage more beautiful and attractive, try to keep the rust out, and place it next to a similar cage, containing another *bird of paradise*: at least that way we don't feel so isolated.

However, has this ever been an altogether happy solution? Our colorful bird remains locked up and is out of its true element. Its true nature is to spread its wings and fly.

How, then, do we get out of this cage? What we, the soul-birds, have to do is to *un-learn* our false self-identification, realizing (not only intellectually) that our true life is formless, timeless, nameless, eternal laughter, without beginning or end. In short, we have to experience Self-realization.

Does this formless goal sound inspiring and promising to you? Or does it perhaps feel a bit too transcendental, too unrealistic, too far from your present reality? In fact, it is not easy for a bird born in a cage to believe that its true nature is to soar freely over brooks and meadows. Likewise, the human mind finds it difficult to imagine its natural freedom in omnipresence. Yet, it is there alone that we will finally find our homeland. But, unfortunately, getting there isn't at all easy.

Freedom is for heroes

Isn't it strange that it should take such effort to return to our natural state? Actually, even much more than just effort is involved. Releasing our soul from ego-consciousness is, in truth, a task for heroes, which requires enormous courage, as it brings about a radical change of identity. The ego, in fact, is mightily scared of losing its habitual sense of bodily identity, and of expanding into something formless, limitless, unknown. Self-remembrance can only be accomplished one little step at a time, simply because we are so accustomed to feeling ourselves as a mortal human being.

* Praecepta Lessons

By daily meditation the cage is gradually opened, if we so want. The bird of paradise then hops outside a short distance, but immediately thinks, "Oh, this vast world!" Terrified, it hops hurriedly back into its cage again. Here it feels secure once more, but remains locked up in a tiny reality.

Daily life, too, tends to push us back into our cage, into this false little identification, as we continuously circle around our ego, thinking "my decision, my satisfaction, my opinion, my difficulty, etc." Our soul is thereby firmly tied to the body and identifies with it.

We have to face the fact that exiting our cage and returning to our blissful soul is an arduous task. But every little effort is precious, since the only way out of suffering is to realize our true Self. And who of us isn't sick of suffering, of failure, of pain, of being hurt, abandoned, betrayed, disillusioned, forgotten?

Once we contact the formless reality, nothing can touch us anymore. And once that formless reality expands, we find ourselves far beyond the inevitable pains of earthy life. Yogananda writes in his *Autobiography of a Yogi*: "If 'escapism' be a need of man, cramped in his narrow personality, can any escape compare with the majesty of omnipresence?"

The door of the cage

How to exit the cage? Where is its door? It is first the spine and then the spiritual eye. We find that door by going "in and up" in meditation. As has been well said: "The only way out is in!"

Yogananda reassures us that, through deepening our meditation, we will get used to the inner flight: "Gradually, then, by repeated sorties, the bird becomes accustomed to being outside its cage. Then finally, one day, it spreads its wings and soars up into the sky, free at last!"* The result is bliss. In that state we are our true selves again. We experience the supreme joy of freedom.

The grace of saints and masters

But alas, in our present state, we still find ourselves in the cage (at least most of us do). Fortunately, great yogis come to assist us with their love, teachings, and grace. More than two thousand years ago, Patanjali, the father of yoga, described in his Yoga Sutras the ten principal attitudes—the *yamas* and

* *The Essence of Self-Realization*

niyamas—which we are required to cultivate, if we want to shift our sense of identity from the little ego to our eternal soul.

One of them is *swadhyaya*, or self-study. Why is *swadhyaya* an essential attitude? And how are we to apply it in our sadhana and daily life?

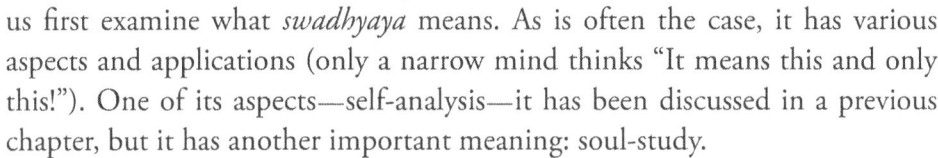

Swadhyaya as soul-contemplation

Before we answer these two questions, let us first examine what *swadhyaya* means. As is often the case, it has various aspects and applications (only a narrow mind thinks "It means this and only this!"). One of its aspects—self-analysis—it has been discussed in a previous chapter, but it has another important meaning: soul-study.

This is Swami Kriyananda's explanation: "Since all the yama-*niyamas* refer more to mental qualities than to outer practices, *swadhyaya* has a deeper meaning than intellectual self-analysis. It is a reference, rather, to ever deeper self-awareness—a process that transcends mental introspection and requires us to see ourselves and everything around us in relation to the higher, divine Self. 'Dwell always,' it tells us, 'in the consciousness of the Self within.'"*

Swami Sri Yukteswar in his book The Holy Science makes this teaching very clear: "*Swadhyaya* is sravana, study, with manana, deep attention, and thereby nididhya, forming an idea of the true faith about the Self; that is, what I am, whence I came, where I shall go, what I have come for, and other such matters concerning the Self."

Sri Yukteswar

So let's practice *swadhyaya* in the way Sri Yukteswar advises: "forming an idea" concerning the questions above. Let's take some time to ponder each answer (through specific quotes by Paramhansa Yogananda), contemplating their meaning in order to gradually absorb "paradise-bird-consciousness" into our being.

* *Awaken to Superconsciousness*

Freedom / 219

"What I am"

Contemplate these words: "I am made of God-substance, since that is the only substance which exists. Therefore I am health; I am success; I am peace."*

"Whence did I come"

Contemplate these words: "All things come from One, all things are sustained in One, and all things are dissolved in One. I will seek the One in the illusion of the many. Life is not worthwhile if it does not breathe in God.... The perfect pattern was set in me in the beginning when man was made after the image of God, as the perfect plan of the plant is enclosed in the tiny seed."†

"Whither shall I go"

Contemplate these words: "Naughty or good, I am Thy child. Sinner or saint, I am Thy child. Since Thy indelible image of perfection is in me, teach me to wipe away the superficial stains of ignorance and know that Thou and I are, and always have been, One... Today I will destroy the image of delusion which desecrates the image of God within me. I will remember that I and my Father are one."‡

"What have I come for"

Contemplate these words: "The purpose of human life is to find God. That is the only reason for our existence... Self-realization is the knowing in all parts of body, mind, and soul that you are now in possession of the kingdom of God; that you do not have to pray that it come to you; that God's omnipresence is your omnipresence; and that all that you need to do is improve your knowing."§

"Because God is perfection, and I am made in His image and likeness, it is my duty to manifest that perfection in all of my endeavors."

---

* *East-West*, October 1933 † *Inner Culture*, Oct.–Dec. 1941 and *East West* Oct. 1933
‡ *Whispers From Eternity*, and *Inner Culture*, April–June 1942 § *The Essence of Self-Realization*

Swadhyaya in our sadhana

Now it's time for practical work. It's time to teach our soul-bird to fly again. Our method of teaching will be one week of specific *sadhana*, or spiritual practices. You can daily practice the sequence given below, or even just a part of it.

The first goal is to help our *bird of paradise* to hop out of the cage every now and then by using powerful Self-realization techniques, practiced with a specific intention.

Yogic techniques can be practiced with many different attitudes, intentions, and purposes. For the coming week, fill every technique with the intention of *swadhyaya* or Self-study: do your best to perceive your formless Self and to identify with it.

> ### The SECRET of MEDITATION is...
> Releasing yourself from
> the limitations of body and ego;
> identifying yourself with Infinity.

Swadhyaya in daily life

The *bird of paradise* needs to learn to fly not only during meditation, but also during daily life.

A word of caution: as we learn to soar inwardly, it is important that during the day we don't become spacey, strange, disconnected, irresponsible, or impractical. *Swadhyaya*, as the great Masters have demonstrated, is always accompanied by having one's feet firmly on the ground. And being strongly grounded and present in your daily activities, experiment with the following practice.

During the day: the detached observer

A perfect daily practice of *swadhyaya* is, with one part of your mind, to remain a detached observer, while you act, work, and relate to others. Try to stay in touch with that part in you which is free, not involved, forever watching. Keep an inward detached smile.

 Swami Kriyananda explains it in this way: "*Swadhyaya* must mean above all self-awareness of some higher kind—awareness of the true Self, surely. The more you become of your own higher Self—that part of you which is not involved in outward activities, but which dwells within you, watching everything that goes on in your life—the more you will approach awareness of the divine within you."*

At night and in the early morning: an affirmation

Daily follow this suggestion by Yogananda: "Every night I will say to myself, 'I am no longer the body; I am the omnipresent Spirit; I am immortal; I am eternal.' And when I awake, I will remember the thought anew."†

Swadhyaya in difficult situations

Difficult situations can become most advantageous if we use them to practice *swadhyaya*. In this way they become an opportunity for our soul to emerge from its cage. Here are some precious affirmations by Yogananda which you can practice.

> **~ During sickness ~**
>
> *Affirm:* "I will always behold in my life the perfect, healthy, all-wise, all-blissful image of God."‡

> **~ During moments of low consciousness ~**
>
> *Affirm:* "In reality I am a son of God.
> I have been dreaming that I am a mortal man,
> but now I am awake. The dream that my soul
> is imprisoned in a bodily cage has vanished.
> My Heavenly Father is the king of the universe.
> I am the heir to all His kingdom of
> power, wealth, and wisdom."§

---

* *Demystifying Patanjali* † *Inner Culture*, April–June 1942 ‡ *Metaphysical Meditations*
§ *Inner Culture*, Jan–March 1941

~ During stress ~

Affirm: "The moment I am agitated, restless, or disturbed in mind, I will retire to silence, discrimination, and concentration, until calmness is restored to my unhappy mind."*

~ During a time of facing obstacles ~

Affirm: "I will realize that God's power is limitless, and, since I am made in His image and likeness, I, too, have power to overcome all obstacles that I may encounter."†

~ During a sense of lack ~

Affirm: "I am the child of the Supreme Spirit. My Heavenly Father possesses everything. Having Him, I have everything, for I own everything that He owns."‡

~ During fear of death ~

Affirm: "The ocean of Spirit has become the little bubble of my little soul. The bubble of my life cannot die, whether floating in birth or disappearing in death in the ocean of Cosmic Consciousness, for I am indestructible consciousness, protected in the bosom of Spirit's immortality."§

* *East-West*, June 1932   † *Inner Culture*, July-Sept 1942   ‡ *Metaphysical Meditations*
§ *Metaphysical Meditations*

~ During tragedy and loss ~

Affirm: "I am the immortal child of God, living for a little while in this mortal body. I am here to behold the tragedies and the comedies of this changeable life with an attitude of unchangeable happiness. I am a child of immortality sent here to play the drama of birth and death, remembering always my deathless Self."*

~ During failure ~

Affirm: "I will transform all conditions, good or bad, into the veritable instruments of success. Before a conquering soul, even dangers loom as benedictions from God."†

~ During moments when the ego is strong ~

Affirm: "Behind the moon is the greater Moon. Behind the sun is the vitality of God. Behind man is the intelligence of God. Therefore I will not limit myself to my ego."‡

~ During worry ~

Affirm: "Today I shall burn the faggots of my worries and fears and kindle the fire of happiness to illumine God's temple within."§

~ During a time of problems ~

Affirm: "I know that as God's child I am perfect. I will recover that consciousness by wisdom and true understanding of the meaning of life and its problems."¶

---

* *Inner Culture*, Jan–March 1941 † *East-West*, Oct 1933 ‡ *Inner Culture*, April, June, 1942
§ *Metaphysical Meditations* ¶ *Inner Culture*, July–Sept 1942

~ During fear ~

Affirm: "I will wipe the dream fears of disease, sadness and ignorance from the soul's face of silence, with the veil of Divine Mother's peace."*

Swadhyaya in a poem

As a final encouragement to spread our wings, let us contemplate one of Yogananda's *Whispers From Eternity*.

I WANT TO BE THY BIRD OF PARADISE

With golden plumes of spiritual unfoldment,
with the softest down of tender feeling,
and decked out in a costume of color and graceful beauty,
I am Thy soul-bird of paradise.

My wings, sped by the eager desire to progress,
beat their way through life's somber skies
in continuous search of the paradise of peace.

Despondency has sometimes daubed dark colors
on the fragile feathers of my bright, sunny mind.

Oh! Bathe me, Thy bird of paradise,
with the cleansing sun-rays of insight, and soothe me
with Thy soft-singing melodies of peace.

Yoga asanas

If you practice the postures, fly this week with **GANAPATIASANA** (*Ganesha's Pose*), feeling that you are hardly touching the ground and you are expanding into the sky. Affirm: **"I sail serenely through skies of inner freedom."** Fly, *bird of paradise*, fly!

---

* *Metaphysical Meditations*

WEEK 7 OF SELF-REALIZATION TRAINING: FREEDOM

Follow this sequence each day:

1) Your training is to **practice** *swadhyaya* in all the techniques as described above.

2) Practice the 20 *body-part recharging*.

3) Optionally practice the yoga asanas, focusing especially on *Ganapatiasana* (Ganesha's Pose).

4) Then follow the standard sequence of the *Hong-Sau* technique (Week 4 of Meditation Training), practicing *Hong-Sau* in the spine or in the spiritual eye. Apply one of the suggestions described in Week 1 of Self-realization Training.

5) Use especially the second phase of meditation (without *Hong-Sau*) for *swadhyaya*: in the inner silence look upward and feel: "I am Spirit, I am pure consciousness."

6) Your second training concerns daily life: try always to **remember your free happy Self.**

Conclusion

Dear friend,

We hope you have reached these last pages of the book already feeling transformed, inspired, and replete within.

Here is one last piece of advice for you: when practicing the *Hong-Sau* technique, try to feel connected to an ancient and noble history, with great sages, with millions of authentic seekers and connected with centuries of yogic culture.

In fact, the *Hong-Sau* technique, as we might remember Yogananda saying, "is one of the greatest contributions of India's spiritual science to the world" and "has been widely practiced in India for more than 7,000 years." There is great power in this tradition, and you too can draw upon it in your meditations.

And even more! This book presents you with the very essence of the yogic tradition, which has always been the practice of "union" (yoga).

As we have seen, our life, our consciousness, our existence, have become disconnected from the great Source of Life. And this separation is the root cause of all our suffering.

Hong-Sau is a yogic remedy for this separation and suffering. Practicing *Hong-Sau* we constantly affirm: "My true Self belongs to Spirit, I am one with Spirit."

May this precious message of the *Hong-Sau* technique spread everywhere in your consciousness, in your body, in your mind, in your heart, helping to heal your inner citizens, bringing them happiness, peace, and harmony. The result will be a feast of union, a celebration of bliss, a joyous triumph of lasting healing.

In his *Whispers from Eternity*, Yogananda describes this state of union (yoga) in a meaningful poem, which is the "Happy End" not only of this book, but also of your inner evolution. Therefore read it slowly, absorbing it deeply, trying to feel the liberating state it conveys. In so doing you will be contacting the very essence of *Hong-Sau*.

With my best wishes for a practice filled with light and blessings,

Jayadev

Thou and I are One

Thy cosmic life and I are one.
Thou art the Ocean,
I am the wave;
We are one.
Thou art the Flame,
I am the spark;
We are one.
Thou art the Flower,
I am the fragrance.
We are one.
Thou art the Father,
I am Thy child;
We are one.
Thou art the Beloved,
I am the lover;
We are one.
Thou art the Lover,
I am the beloved;
We are one.
Thou art the Song,
I am the music;
We are one.
Thou art the Spirit,
I am all nature;
We are one.
Thou art my Friend,
I am Thy friend;
We are one.
Thou art the Master,
I am Thy servant;
We are one.
Thou art my Mother,
I am Thy son;
We are one.

Thou art my Master,
I am Thy disciple;
We are one.
Thou art the Ocean,
I am the drop;
We are one.
Thou art all Laughter,
I am a smile;
We are one.
Thou art the Light,
I am the atom;
We are one.
Thou art Consciousness,
I am the thought;
We are one.
Thou art Eternal Power,
I am strength;
We are one.
Thy peace and I are one.
Thy joy and I are one.
Thy wisdom and I are one.
Thy love and I are one.
That is why Thou and I are one.
Thou and I were one,
and Thou and I will be
   one evermore.

Index of sources

East-West Magazine, 1932–34
Inner Culture Magazine, 1936–42
Paramhansa Yogananda, *Autobiography of a Yogi*, Crystal Clarity Publishers (Original 1946 edition)
Paramhansa Yogananda, *Cosmic Chants*, 1938
Paramhansa Yogananda, *Introduction to Yogoda*, 1923
Paramhansa Yogananda, *Patanjali Lessons*
Paramhansa Yogananda, *Praecepta Lessons*, 1934–38
Paramhansa Yogananda, *Psychological Chart*, 1925
Paramhansa Yogananda, *Whispers from Eternity*, Crystal Clarity Publishers
Paramhansa Yogananda, *Yogoda Lessons*, 1925
Swami Kriyananda, *Affirmations for Self-Healing*, Crystal Clarity Publishers
Swami Kriyananda, *The Art and Science of Raja Yoga*, Crystal Clarity Publishers
Swami Kriyananda, *Awaken to Superconsciousness*, Crystal Clarity Publishers
Swami Kriyananda, *The Beatitudes*, Crystal Clarity Publishers
Swami Kriyananda, *Conversations with Yogananda*, Crystal Clarity Publishers
Swami Kriyananda, *Demystifying Patanjali*, Crystal Clarity Publishers
Swami Kriyananda, *Do It NOW!*, Crystal Clarity Publishers
Swami Kriyananda, *The Essence of Self-Realization*, Crystal Clarity Publishers
Swami Kriyananda, *The Essence of the Bhagavad Gita*, Crystal Clarity Publishers
Swami Kriyananda, *God is for Everyone*, Crystal Clarity Publishers
Swami Kriyananda, *The Hindu Way of Awakening*, Crystal Clarity Publishers
Swami Kriyananda, *In Divine Friendship*, Crystal Clarity Publishers
Swami Kriyananda, *Material Success Through Yoga Principles*, Crystal Clarity Publishers
Swami Kriyananda, *Meditation for Starters*, Crystal Clarity Publishers
Swami Kriyananda, *The New Path*, Crystal Clarity Publishers
Swami Kriyananda, *A Place Called Ananda*, Crystal Clarity Publishers
Swami Kriyananda, *The Promise of Immortality*, Crystal Clarity Publishers
Swami Kriyananda, *Rays of the One Light*, Crystal Clarity Publishers
Swami Kriyananda, *Rays of the Same Light*, Crystal Clarity Publishers
Swami Kriyananda, *The Rubaiyat of Omar Khayyam Explained*, Crystal Clarity Publishers
Swami Kriyananda, *Secrets of Meditation*, Crystal Clarity Publishers
Swami Sri Yukteswar, *The Holy Science*, original 1920 edition

PARAMHANSA YOGANANDA

Born in 1893, Paramhansa Yogananda was the first yoga master of India to take up permanent residence in the West.

He arrived in America in 1920 and traveled throughout the country on what he called his "spiritual campaigns." Hundreds of thousands filled the largest halls in major cities to see the yoga master from India. Yogananda continued to lecture and write up to his passing in 1952.

Yogananda's initial impact on Western culture was truly impressive. His lasting spiritual legacy has been even greater. His *Autobiography of a Yogi*, first published in 1946, helped launch a spiritual revolution in the West. Translated into more than fifty languages, it remains a best-selling spiritual classic to this day.

Before embarking on his mission, Yogananda received this admonition from his teacher, Swami Sri Yukteswar: "The West is high in material attainments but lacking in spiritual understanding. It is God's will that you play a role in teaching mankind the value of balancing the material with an inner, spiritual life."

In addition to *Autobiography of a Yogi*, Yogananda's spiritual legacy includes music, poetry, and extensive commentaries on the Bhagavad Gita, the *Rubaiyat* of Omar Khayyam, and the Christian Bible, showing the principles of Self-realization as the unifying truth underlying all true religions. Through his teachings and his Kriya Yoga path millions of people around the world have found a new way to connect personally with God.

His mission, however, was far broader than all this. It was to help usher the whole world into Dwapara Yuga, the new Age of Energy in which we live. "Someday," Swami Kriyananda wrote, "I believe he will be seen as the *avatar* of Dwapara Yuga: the way shower for a new age."

SWAMI KRIYANANDA

A prolific author, accomplished composer, playwright, and artist, and a world-renowned spiritual teacher, Swami Kriyananda (1926–2013) referred to himself simply as a close disciple of the great God-realized master, Paramhansa Yogananda. He met his guru at the age of twenty-two, and served him during the last four years of the Master's life. He dedicated the rest of his life to sharing Yogananda's teachings throughout the world.

Kriyananda was born in Romania of American parents, and educated in Europe, England, and the United States. Philosophically and artistically inclined from youth, he soon came to question life's meaning and society's values. During a period of intense inward reflection, he discovered Yogananda's *Autobiography of a Yogi*, and immediately traveled three thousand miles from New York to California to meet the Master, who accepted him as a monastic disciple. Yogananda appointed him as the head of the monastery, authorized him to teach and give Kriya initiation in his name, and entrusted him with the missions of writing, teaching, and creating what he called "world brotherhood colonies."

Kriyananda founded the first such community, Ananda Village, in the Sierra Nevada foothills of Northern California in 1968. Ananda is recognized as one of the most successful intentional communities in the world today. It has served as a model for other such communities that he founded subsequently in the United States, Europe, and India.

KRIYACHARYA JAYADEV JAERSCHKY

Jayadev Jaerschky was born in Germany. He began his inner search in his teens and, in 1989, following a pilgrimage to India, he decided to settle in the Ananda center near Assisi and follow the Kriya Yoga tradition of Paramhansa Yogananda as conveyed by his direct disciple Swami Kriyananda. In 1991, he received initiation into Kriya Yoga from Swami Kriyananda, who encouraged him to teach and, later, to write books.

Jayadev holds annual seminars in various parts of Italy. He has also taught in several European countries and in India, Egypt, Russia, Ukraine, and the United States.

In 2007, he founded the European School of Ananda Yoga, of which he is director and where he holds courses throughout the year, training new Ananda Yoga teachers.

Jayadev is the author of numerous books on yoga: *Awakening the Chakras*; *Yoga as a Prayer*; *Kriya Yoga*; etc.

He sings with passion, plays the guitar and has published several music CDs: *Cosmic Chants* (in Italian), *Love God*, *Meditations and Practices with OM* and *Open the Heart Chakra* (the latter two with Peter Treichler).

Every year Jayadev leads a pilgrimage to India, to the sacred places of the Himalayas. The main destination is Badrinath, where Mahavatar Babaji, the supreme master of the Kriya Yoga tradition, is said to reside.

In 2014, Jayadev was appointed Kriyacharya, that is, he was authorized to give the sacred initiation into Kriya Yoga.

FURTHER EXPLORATIONS

CRYSTAL CLARITY PUBLISHERS

If you enjoyed this title, Crystal Clarity Publishers invites you to deepen your spiritual life through many additional resources based on the teachings of Paramhansa Yogananda. We offer books, e-books, audiobooks, yoga, and meditation videos, and a wide variety of inspirational and relaxation music composed by Swami Kriyananda.

See a listing of books below, visit our secure website for a complete online catalog, or place an order for our products

crystalclarity.com | clarity@crystalclarity.com

14618 Tyler Foote Road | Nevada City, CA 95959

800.424.1055

ANANDA WORLDWIDE

Crystal Clarity Publishers is the publishing house of Ananda, a worldwide spiritual movement founded by Swami Kriyananda, a direct disciple of Paramhansa Yogananda. Ananda offers resources and support for your spiritual journey through meditation instruction, webinars, online virtual community, email, and chat.

Ananda has more than 150 centers and meditation groups in over 45 countries, offering group guided meditations, classes, and teacher training in meditation and yoga, and many other resources.

In addition, Ananda has developed eight residential communities in the US, Europe, and India. Spiritual communities are places where people live together in a spirit of cooperation and friendship, dedicated to a common goal. Spirituality is practiced in all areas of daily life: at school, at work, or in the home. Many Ananda communities offer internships during which one can stay and experience spiritual community firsthand.

For more information about Ananda communities or meditation groups near you, please visit ananda.org or call 530.478.7560.

THE EXPANDING LIGHT RETREAT

The Expanding Light is the largest retreat center in the world to share exclusively the teachings of Paramhansa Yogananda. Situated in the Ananda Village community near Nevada City, California, the center offers the opportunity to experience spiritual life in a contemporary ashram setting. The varied, year-round schedule of classes and programs on yoga, meditation, and spiritual practice includes Karma Yoga, personal retreat, spiritual travel, and online learning. Large groups are welcome.

The Ananda School of Yoga & Meditation offers certified yoga, yoga therapist, spiritual counselor, and meditation teacher trainings.

The teaching staff has years of experience practicing Kriya Yoga meditation and all aspects of Paramhansa Yogananda's teachings. You may come for a relaxed personal renewal, participating in ongoing activities as much or as little as you wish. The serene mountain setting, supportive staff, and delicious vegetarian meals provide an ideal environment for a truly meaningful stay, be it a brief respite or an extended spiritual vacation.

For more information, please visit expandinglight.org or call 800.346.5350.

ANANDA MEDITATION RETREAT

Set amidst seventy-two acres of beautiful meditation gardens and wild forest in Northern California's Sierra foothills, the Ananda Meditation Retreat is an ideal setting for a rejuvenating, inner experience.

The Meditation Retreat has been a place of deep meditation and sincere devotion for over fifty years. Long before that, the Native American Maidu tribe held this to be sacred land. The beauty and presence of the Divine are tangibly felt by all who visit here.

Studies show that being in nature and using techniques such as forest bathing can significantly reduce stress and blood pressure while strengthening your immune system, concentration, and level of happiness. The Meditation Retreat is the perfect place for quiet immersion in nature.

Plan a personal retreat, enjoy one of the guided retreats, or choose from a variety of programs led by the caring and joyful staff.

For more information or to make your reservation, please visit meditationretreat.org, email meditationretreat@ananda.org, or call 530.478.7557.

RECOMMENDED READING:
YOGANANDA and KRIYANADA

THE ORIGINAL 1946 UNEDITED EDITION OF YOGANANDA'S SPIRITUAL MASTERPIECE

AUTOBIOGRAPHY OF A YOGI
Paramhansa Yogananda

Autobiography of a Yogi is one of the world's most acclaimed spiritual classics, with millions of copies sold. Named one of the Best 100 Spiritual Books of the twentieth century, this book helped launch and continues to inspire a spiritual awakening throughout the Western world.

Yogananda was the first yoga master of India whose mission brought him to settle and teach in the West. His firsthand account of his life experiences in India includes childhood revelations, stories of his visits to saints and masters, and long-secret teachings of yoga and Self-realization that he first made available to the Western reader.

This reprint of the original 1946 edition is free from textual changes made after Yogananda's passing in 1952. This updated edition includes bonus materials: the last chapter that Yogananda wrote in 1951, also without posthumous changes, the eulogy Yogananda wrote for Gandhi, and a new foreword and afterword by Swami Kriyananda, one of Yogananda's close, direct disciples.

Also available in Spanish and Hindi from Crystal Clarity Publishers.

SCIENTIFIC HEALING AFFIRMATIONS
Paramhansa Yogananda

Yogananda's 1924 classic, reprinted here, is a pioneering work in the fields of self-healing and self-transformation. He explains that words are crystallized thoughts and have life-changing power when spoken with conviction, concentration, willpower, and feeling. Yogananda offers far more than mere suggestions for achieving positive attitudes. He shows how to impregnate words with spiritual force to shift habitual thought patterns of the mind and create a new personal reality.

Added to this text are over fifty of Yogananda's well-loved "Short Affirmations," taken from issues of *East-West* and *Inner Culture* magazines from 1932 to 1942. This little book will be a treasured companion on the road to realizing your highest, divine potential.

METAPHYSICAL MEDITATIONS
Paramhansa Yogananda

Metaphysical Meditations is a classic collection of meditation techniques, visualizations, affirmations, and prayers from the great yoga master, Paramhansa Yogananda. The meditations given are of three types: those spoken to the individual consciousness, prayers, or demands addressed to God, and affirmations that bring us closer to the Divine.

Select a passage that meets your specific need and speak each word slowly and purposefully until you become absorbed in its inner meaning. At the bedside, by the meditation seat, or while traveling—one can choose no better companion than *Metaphysical Meditations*.

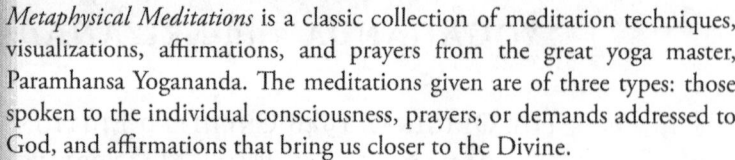

SONGS OF THE SOUL
Paramhansa Yogananda

Yogananda preferred to express his wisdom not in dry intellectual terms but as pure, expansive feeling. To drink his poetry is to be drawn into the web of his boundless, childlike love. In one moment his *Songs of the Soul* invite us to join him as he plays among the stars with his Cosmic Beloved. Then they call us to discover that portion of our own hearts that is eternally one with the Nearest and Dearest. This volume is a bubbling, singing wellspring of spiritual healing that we can bring with us everywhere.

THE NEW PATH
My Life with Paramhansa Yogananda
Swami Kriyananda

Winner of the 2010 Eric Hoffer Award for Best Self-Help/Spiritual Book
Winner of the 2010 USA Book News Award for Best Spiritual Book

The New Path is a moving revelation of one man's search for lasting happiness. After rejecting the false promises offered by modern society, J. Donald Walters found himself (much to his surprise) at the feet of Paramhansa Yogananda, asking to become his disciple. How he got there, trained with the Master, and became Swami Kriyananda makes fascinating reading.

The rest of the book is the fullest account by far of what it was like to live with and be a disciple of that great man of God.

Anyone hungering to learn more about Yogananda will delight in the hundreds of stories of life with a great avatar and the profound lessons they offer. This book is an ideal complement to *Autobiography of a Yogi*.

CONVERSATIONS WITH YOGANANDA
Stories, Sayings, and Wisdom of Paramhansa Yogananda
Recorded with reflections, by his disciple, Swami Kriyananda

For those who enjoyed Paramhansa Yogananda's autobiography and long for more, this collection of conversations offers rare intimate glimpses of life with the Master as never before shared.

This is an unparalleled account of Yogananda and his teachings written by one of his foremost disciples. Swami Kriyananda was often present when Yogananda spoke privately with other close disciples, received visitors and answered their questions, and dictated and discussed his writings. He recorded the Master's words, preserving a treasure trove of wisdom that would otherwise have been lost.

These Conversations include not only Yogananda's words as he spoke them, but the added insight of a disciple who spent over fifty years attuning his consciousness to that of his guru.

The collection features nearly five hundred stories, sayings, and insights from the twentieth century's most famous master of yoga, as well as twenty-five photos—nearly all previously unreleased.

THE ESSENCE OF SELF-REALIZATION
The Wisdom of Paramhansa Yogananda
Recorded, compiled, and edited by his disciple, Swami Kriyananda

Filled with lessons, stories, and jewels of wisdom that Paramhansa Yogananda shared only with his closest disciples, this volume is an invaluable guide to the spiritual life, carefully organized in twenty main topics.

Great teachers work through their students, and Yogananda was no exception. Swami Kriyananda comments, "After I'd been with him a year and a half, he began urging me to write down the things he was saying during informal conversations." Many of the three hundred sayings presented here are available nowhere else. This book and *Conversations with Yogananda* are must-reads for anyone wishing to know more about Yogananda's teachings and to absorb his wisdom.

"Be assured that at each sitting, whether for one page or one chapter, you will have gleaned some refreshment for a tired heart or a thirsty soul. . . . *Essence* is easy to read, besides being quite a bit of fun." —*Spirit of Change Magazine*

WHISPERS FROM ETERNITY
A Book of Answered Prayers
Paramhansa Yogananda
Edited by his disciple, Swami Kriyananda

Many poetic works can inspire, but few have the power to change lives. These poems and prayers have been "spiritualized" by Paramhansa Yogananda: Each has drawn a response from the Divine. Yogananda was not only a master poet, whose imagery here is as vivid and alive as when first published in 1949: He was a spiritual master, an avatar.

He encouraged his disciples to read from *Whispers from Eternity* every day, explaining that through these verses he could guide them after his passing. But this book is not for his disciples alone. It is for spiritual aspirants of any tradition who wish to drink from this fountain of pure inspiration and wisdom.

DEMYSTIFYING PATANJALI: THE YOGA SUTRAS
The Wisdom of Paramhansa Yogananda
Presented by his direct disciple, Swami Kriyananda

For millennia this fascinating series of yoga sutras, or aphorisms, by the great Indian sage Patanjali has baffled scholars and mystics alike. Today, these powerful writings stand newly revealed as a practical, concise handbook that redirects all sincere seekers swiftly towards their true home in the Divine.

Demystifying Patanjali represents the confluence of three great yoga teachers. Patanjali, the first exponent of the ancient teachings of yoga, presented his system of inner contemplation, meditation practice, and ethics. Paramhansa Yogananda, perhaps the greatest of all yoga masters to live and teach in the West, revealed with deep insight the meaning behind Patanjali's often obscure aphorisms. Finally, Yogananda's direct disciple, Swami Kriyananda, the author of nearly 150 spiritual books in his own right, compiled his guru's explanation into a clear, systematic presentation.

These three great souls combine to give us a modern scripture that will enlighten the mind, expand the heart, and inspire the soul of every seeker.

THE ESSENCE OF THE BHAGAVAD GITA
Explained by Paramhansa Yogananda
As remembered by his disciple, Swami Kriyananda

Rarely in a lifetime does a new spiritual classic appear that has the power to change people's lives and transform future generations. This is such a book. This revelation of India's best-loved scripture approaches it from a fresh perspective, showing its deep allegorical meaning and down-to-earth practicality. The themes presented are universal: how to achieve victory in life through union with the Divine; how to prepare for life's final exam — death — and what happens afterward; and how to triumph over all pain and suffering.

Swami Kriyananda worked with Paramhansa Yogananda in 1950 while the Master completed his commentary. At that time, Yogananda commissioned him to disseminate his teachings worldwide.

"Millions will find God through this book!" Yogananda declared upon completion of the manuscript. "Not just thousands—millions. I have seen it. I know."

In this fresh perspective, Swami Kriyananda, direct disciple of Yogananda, explains why the teachings of a religious organization like the Church can be marred by omission, misinterpretation, or a lack of understanding. He then presents Yogananda's "gemstones of Christ's teaching" in all their resplendence.

THE HINDU WAY OF AWAKENING
Its Revelation, Its Symbols: An Essential View of Religion
Swami Kriyananda

Hinduism, as it comes across in this book, is a robust, joyful religion, amazingly in step with the most advanced thinking of modern times, in love with life, deeply human as well as humane, delightfully aware of your personal life's needs, for the teaching in this book is no abstraction: It is down-to-earth and pressingly immediate.

This book brings order to the seeming chaos of the symbols and imagery in Hinduism and clearly communicates the underlying teachings from which these symbols arise.

MATERIAL SUCCESS THROUGH YOGA PRINCIPLES
Swami Kriyananda

Are you satisfied with your life as it is? Do you want to keep pushing forward, armed only with grit and determination? Or would you like to learn how to align your will with the power of the universe?

This book can transform your life at its core. This is the opportunity that stands before you now.

Material Success through Yoga Principles is in a sense, an autobiography of perseverance and loyalty to principle until success is achieved. Swami Kriyananda's own life is proof that these principles work. And the successful lives of thousands he has influenced show that these principles can be of benefit to anyone who learns and uses them.

Many people, Paramhansa Yogananda said, fail to succeed in life for lack of what he called "spiritual adventurousness." Successful people are those who have the imagination, and the courage, to embrace new ways of doing things, even if others scoff, or turn away.

THE WISDOM OF YOGANANDA

Paramhansa Yogananda's timeless wisdom is offered here in an approachable, easy-to-read format. The writings of the Master are presented with minimal editing to capture his expansive and compassionate wisdom, his sense of fun, and his practical spiritual guidance.

How to Be Happy All the Time

Karma and Reincarnation

How to Love and Be Loved

How to Be a Success

How to Have Courage, Calmness, and Confidence

How to Achieve Glowing Health and Vitality

How to Awaken Your True Potential

The Man Who Refused Heaven

How to Face Life's Changes

How to Spiritualize Your Life

How to Live Without Fear

How to Increase Your Magnetism

www.ingramcontent.com/pod-product-compliance
Lightning Source LLC
Chambersburg PA
CBHW081920180426
43200CB00032B/2866